DECONSTRUCTING THEOLOGY

American Academy of Religion

Studies in Religion

28

Editors
Thomas J. J. Altizer
James O. Duke

DECONSTRUCTING THEOLOGY

MARK C. TAYLOR

THE CROSSROAD PUBLISHING COMPANY
&
SCHOLARS PRESS

The Crossroad Publishing Company
575 Lexington Avenue
New York, NY 10022

Scholars Press
101 Salem St., P.O. Box 2268
Chico, CA 95927

Library of Congress Cataloging in Publication Data

Taylor, Mark C., 1945–
    Deconstructing theology.

    (Studies in Religion/American Academy of Religion,
ISSN 0145-2789 ; no. 28)
    1. Theology—Addresses, essays, lectures. 2. Deconstruc-
tion—Addresses, essays, lectures. 3. Theology—19th cen-
tury—Addresses, essays, lectures. 4. Philosophy, Modern—
19th century—Addresses, essays, lectures. I. Title.
II. Series: Studies in Religion (American Academy of
Religion) ; no. 28.
BR50.T34 1982   230'.044   82–5970
ISBN 0–8245–0533–6 (Crossroad Publishing)
ISBN 0–89130–582–3 (Scholars Press)   AACR2

Printed in the U.S.A.

For
Beryl Calvin Taylor

Table of Contents

ACKNOWLEDGMENTS

"Journeys to Moriah: Hegel and Kierkegaard," *Harvard Theological Review* 70 (1977): 305–26.

"*Itinerarium Mentis in Deum*: Hegel's Proofs of God's Existence," *Journal of Religion* 57 (1977): 211–31.

"Toward an Ontology of Relativism," *Journal of the American Academy of Religion* 46 (1978): 41–61.

"Interpreting Interpretation," *Unfinished . . . : Essays in Honor of Ray L. Hart, Journal of the American Academy of Religion Thematic Series* XLVIII/1 (1981): 45–64.

"Tracing," *New Dimensions in Philosophical Theology, Journal of the American Academy of Religion Thematic Series* XLIX/1 (1982): 85–108.

In the buginning is the woid, in the muddle is the sounddance and thereinofter you're in the unbewised again.

James Joyce

... he evolves according to the authors he treats, in order. The inducing object, however, is not the author I am talking about but rather what *he leads me to say about him:* I influence myself *with his permission:* what I say about him forces me to think as much about myself (or not to think as much), etc.

Roland Barthes

Foreword

Deconstructing Theology appears at a moment of profound theological breakdown in the non-Catholic world. Indeed, it appears at a moment, perhaps the ultimate moment, of the breakdown of the theoretical traditions of the West, at least insofar as those traditions have been grounded in human or trans-natural meaning and identity. Thus the project of *Deconstructing Theology* is not one of actual or literal deconstruction, for that has already long since occurred, but rather one of seeking the renewal or rebirth of theology by way of a passage through the end or death of the primal ground of the Western theoretical and theological tradition. This is just the point at which theological thinking is now being reborn, even if reborn in a non-theological form, which is to say a form of thinking that bears no manifest sign of the presence of theology. For it is just that thinking which thinks in response to the end of Western thinking and culture, a thinking which grasps the essential correlation if not unity of the theoretical and theological grounds of the West, which is the deepest and most profound expression of truly modern theology. Such thinking might be said to have begun with Spinoza, but it only realized a comprehensive expression in the nineteenth century, and particularly so in Hegel, Kierkegaard, and Nietzsche. Then it was reborn in the twentieth century, and even reborn in Protestant theology, even if in a birth that proved to be a stillbirth, a birth which soon regressed to a pre-theoretical ecclesiastical form.

The birth of Protestant dialectical theology after the First World War initially offered promise of a genuine modern theology. For it was dialectical in the sense that it sought a full mediation between the God of faith and revelation and the absence or emptiness of God in modern consciousness, society, and experience. Within ten years, however, one of its founders, Karl Barth, had moved from a modern dialectic of faith to a pre-modern analogy of faith, therein moving from a modern to an ecclesiastical theology, a theology whose fundamental norms are derived from the ancient or Reformation confessions of the Church. Another founder of dialectical theology, Paul Tillich, if only in response to his move to America, but also in response to the collapse of democratic socialism, progressively turned away from the modernity which he had initially embraced, and with the third volume of his *Systematic Theology* completed the move from a dialectical to a mediational theology, thereby revealing that the real goal of the latter was a contemporary expression of a traditional ecclesiastical or Church theology. But it was precisely the Church as Church which came to an end in the demise of Christendom, thereby realizing a new and comprehensive sectarian identity, an identity wholly withdrawing it from the modern centers of consciousness and society. We have long since learned that there is no hope of a modern Church theology, at least in the non-Catholic world, and the time has arrived for a renewed modern Protestant or post-ecclesiastical theology, a theology fully situated in the world or worlds of modernity.

Mark C. Taylor is the first American post-ecclesiastical systematic or philosophic theologian, the first theologian free of the scars or perhaps even the memory of Church theology, and the first theologian to address himself solely to the purely theoretical or cognitive problems of theology. All too significantly, Taylor began his professional work with an intensive study of Kierkegaard, the very Kierkegaard who is almost universally regarded as the primal religious thinker of modernity, but also the Kierkegaard who while inspiring the early dialectical Barth, was abandoned by Barth when Barth embarked upon the *Church Dogmatics.* Taylor was not alone in drawing forth a wholly non-ecclesiastical but nevertheless profoundly Christian identity of Kierkegaard, but he was alone in seeking a full theological identity of this Kierkegaard, and he was also alone in his next and inevitable move of wholly correlating Hegel and Kierkegaard, thereby for the first time fully establishing the profoundly modern theological identity of Kierkegaard. Through these studies Taylor has not only recaptured but also recapitulated the actual genesis of modern theology, and done so in an intellectual and cultural situation wherein theology is free of the Church, and thereby free of the very power and ground which theological thinking itself negated in realizing its modern epiphany. Taylor continues this movement in *Deconstructing Theology,* thus inevitably and necessarily extending it to Nietzsche, even while moving into the contemporary world of modern or post-modern thinking.

Ironically, the most powerful presence in Barth's *Romans* commentary is a purely and profoundly religious presence, a presence which had progressively disappeared in the Protestant theologies of the eighteenth and nineteenth centuries, and also a presence which is itself negated in the dialectical movement of this truly dialectical theology. Barth was the deepest and purest religious thinker in the modern Protestant world, thereby he necessarily was a Kierkegaard reborn, but he reversed this dialectical and Kierkegaardian identity in his move to a Church theology, thereby progressively diminishing and dissolving his own religious thinking, and also thereby ironically recapitulating the movement of pre-Barthian and post-Reformation Protestant theology. Tillich also moved in a parallel although more ambivalent manner, and this movement was reenacted comprehensively in twentieth-century Protestant and Catholic theology, so that soon after the Second World War genuine religious thinking was virtually absent

from Christian theology. This was also the historical point at which theology
ceased to be of general cultural or social interest, and sensitive inquirers
were driven to seemingly non-theological arenas to discover the presence of
contemporary religious thinking. For such thinking has continued to be at
hand, it is manifestly present in a large body of modern art, literature, and
music, just as it has also been present in Western investigations of non-
Western religious traditions. Now it is becoming present, or hopefully so, in
post-ecclesiastical and radical theology, a theology which is radical perhaps
because of its renewed religious quest.

So it is that Alpha and Omega, the mythical and the eschatological,
ritual and vision, gradually but decisively move into the center of Taylor's
theological thinking, and do so by way of a necessary theological logic, a
logic embodying a progressive opening to a purely religious ground. This
path will not be strange to a theological student of Hegel's logic, a logic
which made possible both the release and the realization of Kierkegaard's
religious thinking, and it will not be strange to the reader or lover of
Nietzsche and Nietzsche's thinking, which began with a religious movement,
profoundly negated that movement, only to arrive by way of a second and
even deeper negation at a total religious vision and thinking. Nietzsche's
vision of Eternal Recurrence might well be said to be the primal foundation,
and even revelatory or scriptural foundation, of post-Structuralist Deconstruction, and surely nowhere else outside of imaginative literature can we
find a truly modern language which is simultaneously and even thereby a
purely religious language. But if only through Foucault and Derrida, we can
see that Nietzsche's thinking and vision are the inevitable culmination of
Hegelian thinking and logic, and thereby we can become open to the
possibility that it is precisely the purest and most radical thinking which
necessarily and inevitably culminates in a purely religious thinking, a thinking which at that point ceases to be religious as such by way of its
embodiment of a total thinking and vision.

The crucial move in this purely modern thinking is by way of a return to
the primordial ground of Western thinking, but this return is not simply and
only a backward movement of return, it is also a forward movement to a post-
Western and even post-modern universality. Thereby an original and
primordial ground passes into an eschatological ground, an eschatological and
universal ground which is itself the necessary essential and historical
consequence of an original ground which is a pure and active actuality. That
original ground itself became hidden and withdrawn with the very naming of
God and Being, a naming and a thinking which gradually but inevitably
posited and envisioned an intrinsic otherness of God. Such an intrinsic
otherness veiled and obscured an original and primordial totality, even if that
totality returned again and again in the West in apocalyptic, mystical,
imaginative, and revolutionary political forms. But not until the modern
world, not until the disappearance or eclipse of a purely transcendent God or

Being, does an original totality become comprehensively present and actual in the fullness of consciousness and history, a fullness of time which theologically can only be named as an eschatological time and end. It is not accidental that Spinoza, Hegel, and Nietzsche so fully employed an actual theological language, a full theological language that no longer could function or be real in "theology," because "theological" language had ever progressively become a solitary and isolated language, referring to nothing whatsoever outside of itself. But in Spinoza, Hegel, and Nietzsche, to say nothing of their poetic counterparts, "God" language is a comprehensive and total language, a language comprehending, whether positively or negatively, all meaning and identity whatsoever.

Even if Augustine and Dante can now increasingly be seen as fathers of modernity, it is no longer possible to return, whether conceptually or imaginatively, to their actual language and vision. This very fact decisively makes manifest the impossibility of returning to the Bible or to a "biblical" revelation. But the closure of the possibility of a unilinear movement of return also establishes the possibility of a forward movement to a universal or eschatological meaning and identity, an eschatological totality which has dominated if not overwhelmed all of the major and fundamental expressions of modern thinking and the modern imagination. Indeed, it was only in the context of this world of modern eschatological thinking and vision that there occurred the historical discovery of the original eschatological identity of the New Testament, a discovery effected by Blake in imaginative solitude long before it occurred in New Testament scholarship. Even the revelation of Eternal Recurrence which came to Nietzsche at Sils-Maria in 1882 happened before the scholarly discovery of the original historical identity of the Kingdom of God by Weiss and Schweitzer. Nor should we forget that this was the time of the advent of modern art, an art that in dissolving the individual autonomy of nature and humanity called forth a new and total actuality of consciousness and perception.

One decisive sign of the presence of dialectical thinking and vision in the modern world is the presence therein of a movement into the heart of darkness, a religious movement into total darkness or the void, a movement actualizing total darkness or emptiness at the center of consciousness and self-consciousness. Self-consciousness thereby passes into its own integral and inherent otherness, and that otherness is realized as a total otherness, but a total otherness grounded in the center of self-consciousness. Thus the self-estrangement and the self-alienation of self-consciousness is the site of the death of God. Only with the advent of the unhappy consciousness in the modern world does the death of God become comprehensively actual and real, but it is precisely a passage through the actuality and totality of that death that releases a truly new and eschatological totality. While the full conceptual ground of this movement was initially established by Hegel in *The Phenomenology of Spirit*, it was Kierkegaard who first comprehensively and systematically unveiled the interior and religious identity of this movement, and Nietzsche who finally envisioned and enacted an all too modern resurrection of the body which is a full resolution of the actual crucifixion of self-consciousness and Spirit. Only in our time is the mundane world of "theology" being initiated into the actuality of these movements, but that initiation promises a rebirth of theology.

Luther, Pascal, Kierkegaard, Strindberg, Kafka, Barth, and Beckett, to cite but a few seminal names, have given us luminous and overwhelming visions of both the actuality and the necessity of an interior voyage into darkness, a darkness which ever more progressively becomes total or all in all. But Blake, Dostoyevsky, Nietzsche, and Joyce (other names could be cited, particularly from the realms of music and art) have given us visions of a voyage into darkness which is therein and thereby, and precisely therein and thereby, a voyage into light, and a light which is light and darkness at once. This is the point at which revelation, and even biblical revelation, is becoming actual and real in our world, and actual and real in the fullness of consciousness and history. A solitary and interior movement into darkness which culminates with the advent of an apocalyptic totality is surely grounded in the Bible, and manifestly so in Paul, and it may well be the most open way for us to a recovery or renewal of the triumphant eschatological proclamation of Jesus. If so, it would mark the reversal of two millenia of theological thinking, a thinking which annulled and dissolved the Kingdom of God precisely by its thinking of "God." This is the thinking which must be deconstructed to make way for an openness of thinking to the presence and actuality of the Kingdom of God. Perhaps the primary vocation of theology is negative thinking of this order, a negative thinking and a negative theology which negates and deconstructs all that theological thinking which negates and dissolves an eschatological and total presence.

Thomas J. J. Altizer

Pretext

"Etymologically," Roland Barthes reminds us, "the text is a cloth; *textus*, from which text derives, means 'woven'."/1/ "Pretext," which can be traced to the Latin *prae* (before)+*textere* (to weave) means "woven in front of." But "pretext" also means "an ostensible or professed purpose; pretense; excuse [Latin, *praetextus*: outward show, pretense, from the past participle of *praetexere*—to weave in front of, disguise, pretend]." The pretext of a pre-text, therefore, is either the disclosure of the professed purpose of the text, or the weaving of a disguise which stands in front of the text. A "Pretext" inscribed between a "Foreword" and a first word: disclosure or (and) disguise?

What, then, can be the pretext of a book which raises the question of the book? The question of the book is, in large measure, the question of theology (and no less of philosophy). With the disappearance of both Author and author, with the death of God and the erasure of the subject, are books still writable? If we can no longer write of God, or write of God as we once did, then can we any longer write books, or write books as we once did? Insofar as the pretext of the pre-text is to retrace the coherence, integrity, unity, and purpose of the work, the text and its pretext belong to the epoch whose closure is at hand. The subversion of author-ity spells the end of the book—an end which marks either the impossibility or the beginning of writing. What, we must ask, can it possibly mean to write in an authorless world?

Let us begin again. "This (therefore) will not have been a book. Still less, despite appearances, will it have been a collection of [six] 'essays' whose itinerary it would be time, after the fact, to recognize; whose continuity and underlying laws could now at last, with all the insistence required on such occasions, be squarely set forth."/2/ This "Pretext" announces no conclusions, anticipates no result. Rather it raises a residual question, a question of remainder: "*quoi du reste aujourd'hui, pour nous, ici, maintenant, d'un Hegel [et d'un Kierkegaard]?*" This question is at least twofold: Where does the presence of Hegel and Kierkegaard continue to be felt today? What scraps (*philosophiske smuler?*) of theirs remain which might still nourish *us*?

It is difficult to imagine two thinkers who have done more to shape modern and postmodern consciousness than Hegel and Kierkegaard. Nowhere has the significance of their work been more keenly recognized than in France.

Hegel and Kierkegaard have been a constant presence in twentieth-century French thought. Authors as diverse as Bergson, Sartre, Merleau-Ponty, Marcel, Levinas, Bataille, Wahl, Hyppolite, Althusser, Foucault, Deleuze, Kristeva, Lacan, and Derrida draw directly and indirectly on the seminal insights of Hegel and Kierkegaard. One of the most important factors in setting this course for French intellectual life has been a series of extraordinary lectures on Hegel's *Phänomenologie des Geistes* delivered by Alexandre Kojève at L'École des Hautes Études from 1933–1939. Kojève's lectures, collected and published by Raymond Queneau under the title *Introduction à la lecture de Hegel: Leçons sur la Phénomenologie de l'esprit*, have left an indelible imprint upon both the substance and style of French thought. The Hegel who emerges from Kojève's reading of the *Phänomenologie* is an existential Hegel, a Hegel who seems possible only in a post-Hegelian world which knows Kierkegaard, Marx, Nietzsche, Heidegger, and Freud. In place of the world-historical philosopher whose abstract thought dispels the ambiguities and dissolves the tensions of historical existence, Kojève portrays a Hegel who is preoccupied with concrete dilemmas of human experience such as the relationship between death and desire, time and eternity, labor and language, mastery and slavery, negativity and resistance, identity and difference, infinitude and finitude, and totality and dispersal. By underscoring the importance of these themes in Hegel's work, Kojève identifies issues with which French thinkers have struggled ever since. Consider, for example: Sartre's being and nothingness, Merleau-Ponty's language and silence, Marcel's mystery, Levinas's alterity, Wahl's unhappy consciousness, Bataille's transgression, Hyppolite's negativity, Althusser's *problématique*, Foucault's dispersal, Deleuze's difference, Kristeva's desire, Lacan's Other, and Derrida's *différance*. The list could be extended, but the point is clear. *Introduction à la lecture de Hegel* is one of the most influential philosophical works of the twentieth century.

I have deliberately described Kojève's "commentary" on Hegel as a "philosophical work," for it is as much a creative philosophical statement as a rigorous analysis of the text of a formidable precursor. In Kojève's *Introduction*, the line between representation and presentation becomes as obscure as the margin between text and interpretation. Kojève's reading of Hegel results in a new philosophical text which both grows out of and advances beyond its predecessor. Though perhaps not fully aware of his interpretive strategy and its implications, Kojève's work is a striking example of what Harold Bloom labels "misprision"—a creative "misreading" of an antecedent text./3/ The productive interplay of writing and rewriting illustrated in Kojève's text embodies many of the critical insights which shape the style of recent French philosophical discourse.

The substance and style of Kojève's *Introduction* deeply inform what is, in my judgment, the most significant movement in contemporary philosophy—Deconstruction. Although Deconstruction has aroused considerable interest (and hostility) among literary critics, students of religion have yet to appreciate its significance. Philosophers of religion and theologians in particular have failed to recognize the importance of Deconstruction as a resource for creative reflection. Elsewhere I have suggested that Deconstruction is the hermeneutic of the death of God and the death of God is the (a)theology of Deconstruction./4/ The writings of some of the leading French post-structuralists disclose philosophical and theological dimensions of issues central to much of the most radical and creative twentieth-century art, music, and literature. Deconstruction directs our attention to critical problems which merit serious consideration: the death of God, the disappearance of the self, the erasure of the (A)author, the interplay of absence and presence and of silence and speech, the encounter with death, the experience of exile, the insatiability of desire, the inevitability of delay, the burden of totality, the repression of difference, the otherness of Other, the subversion of authority, the end of the book, the opening of textuality, and the advent of writing. By creatively probing problems which haunt the postmodern imagination, Deconstruction identifies questions which contemporary theology and philosophy of religion no longer can avoid.

At the center of the movement which has come to be known as "Deconstruction" is the work of the most important philosopher now writing—Jacques Derrida. Derrida burst upon the philosophical scene in 1967 with the simultaneous publication of three major works: *La Voix et le phénomène*, *L'écriture et la différence*, and *De la grammatologie*./5/ Since that time, he has continued to produce a steady stream of seminal essays and books. In a manner not unlike Kojève, Derrida develops his own point of view through the creative reinterpretation of the writings of leading figures in the western philosophical tradition. Plato, Hegel, Rousseau, Nietzsche, Husserl, Heidegger, Freud, Jabès, and Levinas are among the authors toward whom Derrida directs his deconstructive enterprise. Although Kierkegaard is notably (and probably significantly) absent from the list of authors Derrida examines, Kierkegaard's ghost haunts the project of Deconstruction and indirectly informs much of its discourse. As a matter of fact, issues which lie at the heart of the Hegel-Kierkegaard debate/6/ are nowhere being discussed more suggestively than in Derridean Deconstruction. The question with which we began this "Pretext" is really Derrida's: *"quoi du reste aujourd'hui, pours nous, ici, maintenant, d'un Hegel?"* ("what about the remains of a Hegel today for us here, now?")/7/ In an apparent effort to respond to his own query, Derrida develops a non-book, *Glas*, whose only recognizable antecedent is, as Geoffrey Hartman has argued,/8/ Joyce's *Finnegans Wake*. If *Glas* is still philosophy, it is philosophy of a different order than any which has gone before. I am persuaded that this new "philosophy" harbors a radically new theology, a secular, post-ecclesiastical theology which can both draw on and respond to distinctively postmodern experience.

Derrida's own theological identity has, for the most part, gone unnoticed.

As his response to Emmanuel Levinas (whose major work, *Totality and Infinity: An Essay on Exteriority*, is dedicated to the great French Hegel-Kierkegaard scholar, Jean Wahl) and Edmond Jabès indicates, Derrida's theological stance is profoundly influenced by Lurianic Kabbalism./9/ Derrida's Kabbalism, however, is curiously colored by his reading of that most non-Jewish thinker, Nietzsche, even as his reading of Nietzsche is deeply informed by lingering traces of his Jewish heritage. Followers of Derrida have preferred to overlook the theological and religious aspects of his thought, no doubt suspecting that they represent a vestige of the nostalgia which he criticizes so relentlessly. But Derrideans who disregard such theological issues risk superficiality, just as theologians who ignore Deconstruction risk irrelevance. It would not be too much to say that Deconstruction is postmodernism raised to method. From this perspective, the work of Derrida sheds considerable light on contemporary experience. Despite its overt atheism, postmodernism remains profoundly religious, and this atheistic religiosity offers a promising point of departure for a truly postmodern theology.

The essays which comprise this volume explore many of the features of the current philosophical and theological scene which I have briefly described in these introductory comments. In the first two essays, "Journeys to Moriah" and "*Itinerarium Mentis in Deum*," I begin where I have begun in the past—by rethinking Hegel and Kierkegaard. But now this interpretative undertaking is set within the broader context of theological reformulation. Thus in "Toward an Ontology of Relativism" and "Interpreting Interpretation" I seek to appropriate some of the scraps left by Hegel and Kierkegaard which can still nourish theological and philosophical reflection. The final essays, "The Empty Mirror" and "Tracing," attempt to join contemporary discussion by examining some of the theological and religious themes inherent in Deconstruction.

Writing books, after having absorbed the insights of Deconstruction, is as difficult as writing theology, after having interiorized the death of God. Honesty compels us to admit the possibility that neither task can any longer be completed. Nothing is to be gained, however, by the refusal to confront and to acknowledge the magnitude of the difficulties which contemporary theologians are facing. Perhaps these essays can help to clarify the nature and scope of these difficulties and can serve to increase awareness of sources of philosophical insight which theologians so far have failed to tap. It is, of course, undeniable that not only this "Pretext," but this entire volume remains a Pretext—a pre-text to a text yet to be written . . . a postmodern atheology.

Notes

/1/   Roland Barthes, "From Work to Text," *Textual Strategies: Perspectives in Post-Structural Criticism*, ed. J. V. Harari (Ithaca: Cornell University Press, 1979), p. 76.

/2/   Jacques Derrida, *Dissemination*, trans. Barbara Johnson (Chicago: University of Chicago Press, 1981), p. 3.

/3/   See, *inter alia*: *A Map of Misreading* (New York: Oxford University Press, 1975); *Poetry and Repression: Revisionism from Blake to Stevens* (New Haven: Yale University Press, 1976); and *The Anxiety of Influence: A Theory of Poetry* (New York: Oxford University Press, 1973).

/4/   "Text as Victim," *Deconstruction and Theology* (New York: Crossroad, 1982).

/5/   These works have all been translated: *Speech and Phenomena and Other Essays on Husserl's Theory of Signs*, trans. David Allison (Evanston: Northwestern University Press, 1973); *Writing and Difference*, trans. Alan Bass (Chicago: University of Chicago Press, 1978); and *Of Grammatology*, trans. G. C. Spivak (Baltimore: Johns Hopkins University Press, 1976).

/6/   For a detailed discussion of Hegel and Kierkegaard, see my *Journeys to Selfhood: Hegel and Kierkegaard* (Berkeley: University of California Press, 1980).

/7/   Jacques Derrida, *Glas* (Paris: Editions Galilée, 1974), p. 7.

/8/   See: *Saving the Text: Literature/Derrida/Philosophy* (Baltimore: Johns Hopkins University Press, 1981).

/9/   See: Thomas J. J. Altizer, "History as Apocalypse," *Deconstruction and Theology*.

Journeys to Moriah:
Hegel vs. Kierkegaard

Abraham, born in Chaldaea, had in youth already left a fatherland in his father's company. Now, in the plains of Mesopotamia, he tore himself free altogether from his family as well, in order to be a wholly self-subsistent, independent man, to be an overlord himself. . . . The same spirit which had carried Abraham away from his kin led him through his encounters with foreign peoples during the rest of his life; this was the spirit of self-maintenance in strict opposition to everything—the product of this thought raised to be the unity dominant over the nature which he regarded as infinite and hostile (for the only relationship possible between hostile entities is mastery of one by the other). With his herds Abraham wandered hither and thither over a boundless territory without bringing parts of it any nearer to him by cultivating and improving them. . . . The groves which often gave him coolness and shade he soon left again; in them he had theophanies, appearances of his perfect Object on High, but he did not tarry in them with the love which would have made them worthy of Divinity and participant in Him. He was a stranger on earth, a stranger to the soil and to men alike. (Hegel, 1971:185–86)

One cannot weep over Abraham. One approaches him with a *horror religiosus*, as Israel approached Mount Sinai.—If then the solitary man who ascends Mount Moriah, which with its peak rises heaven-high above the plain of Aulis, if he be not a somnambulist who walks securely above the abyss while he who is stationed at the foot of the mountain and is looking on trembles with fear and out of reverence and dread dare not even call to him—if this man is disordered in his mind if he had made a mistake! (Kierkegaard, 1970:71–72)

I. Horror—Horror Religiosus?

Hegel had an uncanny ability to anticipate insights and criticisms of many of his most influential successors. His formulation of positions later developed by left-wing critics such as Marx, Feuerbach, and Bauer, as well as right-wing supports such as Martensen, Heiberg, and Göschel is widely recognized and well documented./1/ Less frequently noted is Hegel's anticipation of important dimensions of Kierkegaard's philosophical and theological perspective. This oversight is largely the result of the failure of partisan commentators to recognize the complexity and the dialectical character of the Hegel-Kierkegaard relationship. We shall attempt to probe more deeply the theological and philosophical issues joining and separating Hegel and Kierkegaard by analyzing their alternative interpretations of Abraham.

Kierkegaard's discussion of Abraham forms the foundation of one of his best known and most popular works, *Fear and Trembling*. In this essay, Kierkegaard at once seeks to ascertain the religious significance of his personal experience and to elaborate a clearly articulated view of faithful existence. Abraham, journeying in lonely silence to Moriah to sacrifice Isaac to the transcendent Lord, represents the knight of faith in whom individual self-fulfillment is actualized most completely. Kierkegaard's entire authorship is unified by a consistent dialectical progression toward the authentic form of existence expressed in the life of Abraham./2/

Hegel's early writings present a picture of Abraham that bears a striking resemblance to Kierkegaard's analysis in *Fear and Trembling*./3/ As always in such cases, the similarities and differences between Hegel and Kierkegaard are complex. While they agree about the main contours of the form of life embodied in Abraham, their interpretations of the significance of Abraham differ widely. In contrast to Kierkegaard's view of Abraham as the paradigm of authenticity, Hegel maintains that Abraham represents the extreme of alienation (later identified as unhappy consciousness) which is the propaedeutic to the reconciliation disclosed in the incarnation. Hegel's entire philosophical system is unified by a consistent dialectical progression that seeks to sublate the inauthentic form of selfhood expressed in the life of Abraham.

Both Kierkegaard and Hegel approach Abraham in horror. For Kierkegaard's persona, Johannes de Silentio, this is a *horror religiosus* generated when he beholds the strenuous life of faith. For Hegel, this is a *horror* that arises from the encounter with the terrible tension of estrangement.

II. Faithful Wandering

In order to appreciate the significance of Hegel's interpretation of Abraham, it is helpful to place his analysis within the context of his early reflection and writing. During his student days at the Tübingen Stift, Hegel fell under the sway of Kantian philosophy. To Hegel and his classmates Hölderlin and Schelling, the coincidence of Kant's critical philosophy and events surrounding the French Revolution seemed to herald the dawn of a new epoch in human history. The principles of freedom and rationality elaborated with theoretical precision in Kant's three critiques appeared to be achieving concrete historical expression in the revolutionary struggle in France. The pervasive influence of Kant on Hegel's thinking throughout the 1790s is evident in his earliest writings. An essay of 1795 entitled "The

Positivity of the Christian Religion" and *The Life of Jesus* (1795) disclose Hegel's attempt to uncover a completely rational religion that lies fully within the bounds of reason and is unencumbered by historical and revelational positivity. In the former manuscript, Hegel presents Christianity as a totally positive religion that has fallen from the moral purity essential to the faith of its founder. *The Life of Jesus* complements the positivity essay by attempting to present Jesus as a thoroughgoing Kantian moralist.

By the time of "The Spirit of Christianity and Its Fate" (1799), Hegel's position has changed significantly./4/ The contact with outstanding leaders of the German romantic movement in Frankfurt and Jena forced Hegel to reevaluate Kant's philosophy./5/ Rather than seeing rational morality as the fulfillment of selfhood, Hegel now maintains that obedience to the moral law perpetuates the inward distention of the personality characteristic of alienation. This interpretation of Kantian morality enables Hegel to reconsider Christianity. In this essay, Jesus emerges as the proponent of a religion of love that stands in marked tension with pure morality. Moreover, the paradigm of positivity no longer is Christianity, but now is Judaism. It is within this context that Hegel elaborates his interpretation of Abraham./6/ Hegel insists that Abraham is the quintessential expression of the spirit of Judaism./7/

"The Spirit of Christianity and Its Fate" is the first significant anticipation of Hegel's mature position. The discussion of love represents a decisive advance beyond the perspective of the Enlightenment and foreshadows pivotal Hegelian notions such as *Geist* and *Vernunft*. In addition to this, the essay contains the rudiments of the dialectical structure upon which Hegel's philosophical system is built. One cannot understand Hegel's view of Abraham apart from the dialectical progression of the essay. Abraham plays a central role in the story of the movement of human spirit from innocence through alienation to reconciliation.

Hegel presents the faith of Abraham as a response to the conflict engendered by the separation of human consciousness from its natural milieu, mythically depicted in the Old Testament flood narrative. Prior to the estrangement of man from nature, Hegel posits a state of harmonious unification in which humankind finds itself at home in, or at one with, its world. With the unleashing of dissolutive flood waters, "Formerly friendly or tranquil nature abandoned the equipose of her elements, requited the faith the human race had in her with the most destructive, invincible, irresistible hostility" (Hegel, 1971:182). Hegel suggests three alternative reactions to the breach between man and nature. The characteristic Greek response is captured by the beautiful pair, Deucalion and Pyrrha, who, "after the flood in their time, invited men once again to friendship with the world, to nature, made them forget their need and their hositility in joy and pleasure, made a peace of *love*, were the progenitors of more beautiful peoples, and made their age the mother of newborn natural life which maintained its bloom of youth" (1971:185–86). In contrast to this effort to restore harmony lost, the Jewish reaction to the flood maintains the hostility between man and nature by attempting to establish human mastery over natural forces. Two possibilities of mastery emerge. Nimrod "persuaded men that they had acquired all good things for themselves and by their own courage and strength" (1971:184), and hence could dominate nature by means of their own activity. Uncertain of the efficacy of human agency, Noah sought mastery over nature through a product of his own reflection.

> It was in a thought-product that Noah built the shattered world together again: his thought-produced ideal [*gedachtes Ideal*] he turned into a [real] Being and then set everything else over against it, so that in this opposition realities were reduced to thoughts, i.e., to something mastered. This Being promised to him to confine within their limits the elements which were his servants, so that no flood was ever again to destroy mankind. (1971:183)/8/

Abraham rendered explicit the implications of Noah's attempted resolution of the human dilemma brought by the severance from the natural domain.

Abraham's entire existence was testimony to his devotion to the radically transcendent Lord who is the ground of all reality./9/ Having suffered separation from the natural whole of which he had been an integral member,

> Mastery was the only possible relationship in which Abraham could stand to the infinite world opposed to him; but he was unable to make this mastery actual, and it therefore remained ceded to his Idea. He himself also stood under his Ideal's domination, but the Ideal was present in his mind, he served the Idea, and so he enjoyed his Ideal's favor; and since its divinity was rooted in his contempt for the whole world, he remained its only favorite. (1971:188–89)

This is a particularly rich passage and requires considerable comment. Rather than seeking immediate reconciliation with the totality from which he had fallen, Abraham tried to establish a domination over the surrounding world that was mediated by an exclusive relation to the Lord of nature and history. Hegel expresses the heart of Judaism represented in Abraham as "the spirit of self-maintenance in strict opposition to otherness" (1971:186)./10/ There were, however, multiple oppositions requisite for Abraham's self-maintenance. On the most basic level, there was the opposition between man and nature (consciousness and world, subject and object) that initiated the movement toward the reintegration of opposites. In addition to this, there was the opposition between God and world, creator and created, master and mastered. Hegel explains:

> The whole world Abraham regarded as simply his opposite; if he did not take it to be a nullity, he looked on it as sustained by the God who was alien to it. Nothing in nature was supposed to have any part in God; everything was simply under God's mastery. (1973:187)

Through the relationship to God, Abraham attempted to maintain himself in opposition to the hostile powers of nature./11/ In this process a further opposition emerged. As a member of the created order, Abraham stood opposed to the wholly other God upon whom he was absolutely dependent. The positive relation to the divine for which Abraham longed could be established only by unqualified obedience to God expressed in a thoroughly negative relation to world and to self. Negation of world and self and affirmation of God stood in a completely dialectical relationship. From this perspective, it becomes apparent that the Abrahamic "solution" to the alienation of man from nature replaced one form of slavery with a more profound servitude. The price of the mastery over nature was bondage to a transcendent Lord whose demands upon the individual are infinite.

Abraham's heteronomous obedience to transcendent authority deepened his separation from and heightened his opposition to this world. Hegel points out that "The first act which made Abraham the progenitor of a nation was a disseverance which snapped the bonds of communal life and love. The entirety of the relationships in which he had hitherto lived with men and nature, these beautiful relationships of his youth he spurned" (1971:185). Abraham became a faithful wanderer, a lonely nomad who "was a stranger on earth, a stranger to men and soil alike. Among men he always was a foreigner" (1971:196). The struggle to avoid constricting ties to the surrounding world sometimes became violent. At certain junctures in Jewish history, obedience to God manifested itself in the effort to slay infidels. For Abraham, the supreme test of faith was his willingness to obey the divine demand to sacrifice his own son. Only in such an extraordinary act of negation could complete devotion to God be affirmed. Anticipating his discussion of Christianity, Hegel writes:

> Love alone was beyond his [Abraham's] power; even the one love he had, his love for his son, even his hope of posterity—the one mode of extending his being, the one mode of immortality he knew and hoped for—could depress him, trouble his all-exclusive heart and disquiet it to such an extent that even this love he once wished to destroy; and his heart was quieted only through the certainty of the feeling that this love was not so strong as to render him unable to slay his beloved son with his own hand. (1971:187)

From the viewpoint represented by Abraham, self-realization is inextricably bound to religious faith. Individual selfhood is most completely actualized in the isolation from other persons and the opposition to the natural realm established by total devotion/12/ to the transcendent Lord over against whom the individual always stands. This is the end toward which "the spirit of self-maintenance in strict opposition to everything" is directed.

What for Abraham was the goal of human striving, is for Hegel the negative moment of alienation which must itself be negated if reconciliation is to become actual. Rather than healing the breach between man and nature, Abraham's type of faith exacerbates the opposition between the individual and his social and natural world. The faithful wanderer remains alienated from his natural environment and from the rest of the human race. Even the ostensibly sustaining relationship to God really represents a further dimension of estrangement. God remains other—wholly other— apart from and opposed to finite persons. Moreover, the infinity of the demands placed upon the individual by this authoritarian Master necessarily renders reconciliation between self and God eschatological./13/ This leads to the final and most excruciating aspect of alienated existence—the alienation of the self from itself. Unable to fulfill completely the commandments of the Lord, the believer becomes guilty. He is not what he ought to be. Reality and ideality clash in his own personality and perpetuate precisely the inward tension he has been attempting to overcome. As Hegel later points out in the *Phänomenologie des Geistes,*

> we have here that dualizing of self-consciousness within itself, which lies essentially in the notion of mind; but unity of the two elements is not yet present. Hence the *unhappy consciousness,* the alienated soul which is the consciousness of self as a divided nature, a doubled and merely contradictory being. (1967:251)

Self against nature, self against selves, self against God, self against itself— the unhappy consciousness that is the fate of Abrahamic faith. Judaism, Jean Hyppolite explains, "poses essence beyond existence and God outside of man. By recognizing the duality of the extremes, I stand with the nonessential. I am merely nothingness; my essence is transcendent. But that my essence is not in me but posed outside of me necessarily entails an effort on my part to rejoin myself so as to free myself from nonessence. Human life, thus, is an unceasing effort to attain itself. But this effort is futile, because immutable consciousness is posed as transcendent *a principio,*" (Hyppolite, 251). Put more briefly, for Abraham, "melancholy, unfelt unity was the supreme reality" (1971:194). Hegel summarizes his interpretation of Abraham when he suggests that the guiding principle of the Jewish religion

> was the spirit inherited from its forefathers, i.e., was the infinite object [*das unendliche Objekt*], the essence [*der Inbegriff*] of all truth and all relations, which thus is strictly the sole infinite subject, for the object can only be called 'object' in so far as man with the life given him is presupposed and called the living or the absolute subject. This, so to say, is the sole synthesis; the antitheses are the Jewish nation, on the one hand, and, on the other, the world and all the rest of the human race. These antitheses are the genuine pure objects; i.e., this is what they become in contrast with an existent, an infinite, outside them; they are without intrinsic worth and empty, without life; they are not even something dead—a nullity [*ein Nichts*]—yet they are a something only is so far as the infinite object makes them something, i.e., makes them not something which is, but something *made* which for itself has no life, no rights, no love. (1971:191)

As we have noted, however, Hegel's analysis of Abraham cannot be understood apart from the dialectical progression of the essay as a whole. Hegel insists that Abraham's faith and the Jewish religion are moments in the unfolding of human spirit that prepare the way for the more complete form of selfhood revealed in Christianity. From emptiness comes fullness; from bondage, freedom; from alienation, reconciliation.

III. Faithful Communion

Jesus, Hegel argues, set himself against the entire spirit and fate of the Jewish religion. Whereas Judaism emerged from the negation of primordial unity, Jesus proclaimed the negation of this negation which reconciles or reintegrates self and other in harmonious interrelationship.

> Over against commands which required a bare service of the Lord, a direct slavery, an obedience without joy, without pleasure or love, i.e., the commands in connection with the service of God, Jesus set their precise opposite, a human urge and so a human need. Religious practice is the most holy, the most beautiful, of all things; it is our endeavor to unify the discords necessitated by our development and our attempt to exhibit the unification in the *ideal* as fully *existent*, as no longer opposed to reality, and thus to express and confirm it in a deed. (1971:206)

Each of the discords perpetuated by Abraham's faith is overcome in the religion of Jesus. To see how this is so, it is necessary to return to the *telos* of the Jewish spirit.

We have argued that the alienation inherent in Abraham's form of existence finds its most profound expression in the self's opposition to itself. Unable to fulfill God's law, the individual becomes guilty, thereby deepening his separation from and establishing his opposition to the Lord. As the previous text suggests, Hegel believes this alienation to be inseparable from the servility of such a God-self or Master-slave relationship. Recalling the significant influence Kant exercised on Hegel's thought during this period, we might suspect Hegel to oppose this positivistic, authoritarian faith and heteronomous legality with a rational faith and an autonomous morality. As we have noted, this is precisely the line of argument developed in "The Positivity of the Christian Religion." But by 1798, Hegel thinks that Kant's position preserves and does not resolve the dilemma of self-alienation. He goes so far as to suggest that Kantian morality is an extension of the spirit of Judaism. By absolutizing the distinction between universal, rational moral law and idiosyncratic, natural inclination, Kant internalizes the man/nature opposition in a way that necessitates the self's opposition to itself. The essential difference between the heteronomous obedience of Abraham and the autonomous conduct of the Kantian moralist is not that the former enslaves himself, while the latter is free, but that the former has his lord outside himself, while the latter carries his lord in himself. Even the purest moral striving leads to continued self-alienation: particularity set against universality, inclination against obligation, desire against duty, passion against reason, self against self.

Hegel maintains that Jesus represents "a spirit raised above morality." The Sermon on the Mount, Hegel argues, "does not teach reverence for the laws; on the contrary, it exhibits that which fulfills the law and makes law superfluous" (1971:212). Love emerges as the means by which the law, Jewish or Kantian, is simultaneously fulfilled and annulled. Through love intrapersonal disintegration is sublated by the integration of inclination and obligation. Since the lover *wants* to fulfill his obligation to the beloved, desire and duty do not oppose one another. Discussing love in a passage that indicates his early disaffection with Kant's moral philosophy, Hegel suggests:

> the inclination [to act as the laws may command], a virtue, is a synthesis in which the law (which, because it is universal, Kant always calls something 'objective') loses its universality and the subject its particularity; both lose their opposition, while in the Kantian conception of virtue this opposition remains, and the universal becomes the master and the particular the mastered. . . . In the 'fulfillment' of both the laws and duty, their concomitant, however, the moral disposition, etc. ceases to be the universal opposed to the law, and therefore this correspondence of law and inclination is life, and, as the relation of differents to one another, [is] love. . . . (1971:214–15)/14/

Love unifies the personality by reconciling the is and the ought within the self.

Love, however, is not simply an intrasubjective phenomenon. The cultivation of a loving disposition leads to the reunification of the self with its natural and social world. Reflecting the influence of the romantics, Hegel contrasts to the desacralized world of the Jewish religion/15/ a cosmos sacralized by the omnipresence of the divine. Hegel contends that the truth disclosed in the incarnation is the coinherence of the infinite and finite. God is immanent in, and not radically transcendent to the world. Given the mutual indwelling of the infinite and the finite, the relationship of the finite to the infinite presupposes the affirmation and not the negation of the finite. Jesus proclaimed that "nature is holier than the temple" devoted to an alien God (1971:208). In more general terms, Jesus insisted that the individual is not to withdraw from, but is to become involved with the ongoing worldly process. Reconciliation is impossible apart from the restitution of unity with the natural determinants of existence, both within (i.e., sensuous inclination) and without the self.

With respect to the individual's social world, Hegel's contention that love is the means by which alienation is negated implies that self-reconciliation must be mediated by reconciliation with other selves. Against the individualism of Abraham in which self-identity is maintained by virtue of opposition to otherness, Hegel argues, selfhood is inherently social; self-identity is fully relational. Professor Stephen Crites points out that "although lovers remain distinct from one another, they are no longer foreign to one another, no longer in opposition to one another, no longer mutually limiting as mere objects are" (30). In love, selves overcome isolated individuality and abstract opposition, and maintain self-identity through relationship to each other. Borrowing the organic metaphor that had been revitalized by nineteenth-century romantics, Hegel suggests that "each separate lover is one organ in a living whole" (1971:308). The whole, of course, is nothing other than the relationship itself. The members, in this case, the lovers, both sustain and are sustained by their relationship. Organs and organism, lovers and love, relata and relationship have no independent reality, but live only in and through each other.

The difficult point to understand in the complex analysis of the nature of relationship that grows out of Hegel's examination of love is that relationship is at once the source of unity and distinction. Separation of self and other need not imply hostile opposition, but can entail a distinction that is simultaneously a unification. Hyppolite's analysis again is helpful: "Love is the miracle through which two become one without, however, completely suppressing the duality. Love goes beyond the categories of objectivity and makes the essence of life actually real by preserving difference within union." (164). Self and other are joined in a substantial unity that also establishes their determinate distinction from one another. Love presupposes both the unity of and the difference between the lovers. When the purely dialectical character of this relationship is grasped, we can see the basis of Hegel's contention that self-reconciliation must be mediated by the reconciliation with other. From the lovers' perspective, genuine self-realization is impossible apart from the relationship to each other. The particular identity of the lover grows out of the association with the beloved. Self-identity and relation-to-other are not exclusive opposites as Abraham had supposed, but in the final analysis, are inseparable. Lovers find themselves in each other, and in so doing, sublate each other's otherness or foreign character. Relationship to each other is at the same time self-relation. In love lordship and bondage, domination and submission, give way to mutuality and communion.

> In contrast to the Jewish reversion to obedience, reconciliation in love is a liberation; in contrast to the re-recognition [*der Weideranerkennung*] of lordship, it is the cancellation of lordship in the restoration of the living bond, of that spirit of love and mutual faith which, considered in relation to lordship, is the highest freedom. This situation is [for the Jew] the most incomprehensible opposite of the Jewish spirit. (1971:241)

This freedom in, and not from, relationship is, for Hegel, genuine freedom—the abrogation of heteronomy and the achievement of autonomy. A unity that sustains distinction, and distinction that generates unity. Twoness-in-oneness and oneness-in-twoness; identity-within-difference; the

miracle of love . . . the fulfillment of selfhood. Hegel identifies this faithful
communion of loving individuals with the Kingdom of God.

> What Jesus calls the 'Kingdom of God' is the living harmony of men, their
> fellowship in God; it is the development of the divine among men, the rela-
> tionship with God which they enter through being filled with the Holy Spirit;
> i.e., that of becoming his sons and living in the harmony of their developed
> many-sidedness and their entire being and character. In this harmony their
> many-sided consciousness chimes with one spirit and their many different
> lives with one life, but, more than this, by its means the partitions against
> other godlike beings are abolished, and the same living spirit animates the
> different beings, who therefore are no longer merely similar but one; they
> make up not a collection [eine Versammlung] but a communion [eine
> Gemeine], since they are unified not in a universal, a concept . . . , but
> through life and through love. (1971:277–78)

This text both underscores the intersubjective character of Hegel's
interpretation of authentic selfhood and points toward the final dimension of
alienation negated by love—toward the reconciliation of self and God.
Hegel's exploration of love leads to the conclusion that love, which "excludes
all opposition and neither restricts nor is restricted, is not finite at all," but is
infinite (1971:304). In other words, love is divine, or God *is* love. Hegel
agrees with 1 John 4:16: "God is love and anyone who lives in love lives in
God, and God lives in him." It should be clear that Hegel believes Jewish
and Christian notions of God and of the God-self relation to be polar opposites./16/ From Jesus' point of view, God can never be an "infinite Object,"
for between man and God, there is no "cleft of objectivity and subjectivity;
one is to the other an other only in that one recognizes the other; both are
one" (1971:265). Hegel reiterates this important point when he delineates
the conditions of the possibility of faith.

> 'God is spirit, and they who worship him must worship him in spirit and in
> truth.' How could anything but a spirit know a spirit? The relation of spirit to
> spirit is a feeling of harmony, is their unification [Vereinigung]; how could
> heterogeneity be unified? Faith in the divine is only possible if in the believer
> himself there is a divine element which rediscovers itself, its own nature, in
> that on which it believes, even if it be unconscious that what it has found *is*
> its own nature. (1971:266)/17/

The faithful appropriation of the identity of the infinite and the finite, the
divine and the human, God and self, is the negation of the last vestige of
alienation and brings complete atonement.

In sum, love opposes opposition, negates negation. It is the power that
reconciles the opposites left sundered in Abraham's faith. Hegel concludes
that love "deprives man's opposite of all foreign character, and discovers life
itself without any further defect. In love the separate does still remain, but
as something united and no longer as something separate; life [in the subject]
senses life [in the object]" (1971:305). In love, self and other, subjectivity and

objectivity, are unified. "Only through love is the might of objectivity broken, for love upsets its whole sphere" (1971:247). Or as Hegel states tersely elsewhere, "in love alone are we at one with the object, so that there is no mastery or being mastered."/18/ Self at one with nature, with selves, with God, with itself—the peace of atonement, the joy of unity regained. Faithful communion rather than faithful wandering./19/

IV. Faithful Solitude

While Hegel regards Abraham's form of life as the estrangement Christian belief seeks to overcome, Kierkegaard views Abraham as the ideal knight of faith in whom authentic selfhood is ideally represented. As with Hegel, Kierkegaard's argument cannot be grasped adequately apart from the context within which he places his interpretation of Abraham. *Fear and Trembling* is an integral part of Kierkegaard's intricate pseudonymous authorship. Throughout this authorship, Kierkegaard carefully charts the dialectical progression from less to more complete forms of selfhood. By means of various personae, he explores different stages on life's way. Each pseudonym presents an ideal personality type that embodies a particular "life-view" [*Livs-Anskuelse*]. The alternative life-views or stages are neither randomly selected nor arranged, but grow out of Kierkegaard's analysis of the structure and development of the self. In a manner reminiscent of Hegel, the Kierkegaardian dialectic of existence includes three fundamental moments: the aesthetic, the ethical, and the religious./20/ There is a striking similarity in the formal structure and progression described by Hegel and Kierkegaard./21/ As early as "The Spirit of Christianity and Its Fate," Hegel had identified the dialectical structure that underlies his entire system.

> The culmination of faith, the return to the Godhead whence man is born, closes the circle of man's development. Every thing lives in the Godhead, every living thing is its child, but the child carries the unity, the connection, the concord with the entire harmony, undisturbed though undeveloped, in itself. It begins with faith in gods outside oneself, with fear, until through its actions it has [isolated and] separated itself more and more; but then it returns through associations to the original unity which is now developed, self-produced, and sensed as a unity. The child now knows God, i.e., the spirit of God is present in the child, issues from its restrictions, annuls the modification, and restores the whole. God, the Son, the Holy Spirit! (1971:273)

As our analysis of Hegel's view of Abraham has disclosed, Hegel plots the movement from the harmonious though undifferentiated unification of self and other (i.e., nature, selves, God, and self), through the negation of this unity and the development of differentiation, alienation, and opposition, to the final stage of reintegration in which self and other are reconciled in a unity that maintains, rather than negates, difference. The *telos* renders explicit what was implicit in the *archē*. But the end is not simply a return to the beginning, for in the process individual selfhood emerges as self-conscious and comes to recognize its internal relation to the totality in and through which it gains determinate identity. It is clear that in his early writings, Hegel understands the Jewish spirit to play a pivotal role in this dialectic. Abraham represents the negative moment of estrangement that lies between primordial and restored harmony. Abraham wanders between the Garden and the Kingdom. Since Hegel is convinced that ontogeny recapitulates phylogeny,/22/ Abraham becomes the estranged Everyman.

Kierkegaard's dialectic of existence follows the general direction mapped in the first two moments of Hegel's analysis. The movement through the Kierkegaardian stages is marked by the increasing differentiation of self and other by which individual selfhood achieves its most radical expression. For Kierkegaard, the whole pathos of human striving is directed to the clear delineation of the individual vis-à-vis the natural and social environment and over against the wholly other God. Kierkegaard believes that the third moment of the Hegelian dialectic is in fact a return to the nondifferentiation characteristic of the first moment./23/ In other words, Hegel's effort to reintegrate self and other negates the very individuality in which Kierkegaard sees authenticity. The identity peculiar to realized selfhood is established and maintained through contrast with and opposition to otherness. Instead of representing an intermediate stage between innocence and redemption (i.e., a negative moment that must be negated), Kierkegaard's Abraham is the model of realized individuality (i.e., the positive moment that must be affirmed). In order to understand more fully Kierkegaard's view of Abraham, and to gain a better sense of the similarities joining and differences separating Hegel and Kierkegaard, it will be helpful to consider briefly each of Kierkegaard's stages of existence.

The aesthetic stage consists of two forms of life that stand in polar tension: immediacy and reflection. Drawing on the image of the maturing child, Kierkegaard writes:

> And yet child-life and youth-life are dream-life, for the innermost thing, that which in the deepest sense is man, slumbers. The child is completely turned outward, its inwardness is extroversion, and to that extent the child is wide awake. But for a man, to be awake means to be eternally turned inward in inwardness, and so the child is dreaming, it dreams itself sensuously at one with everything [*drømmer sig sandseligt sammen med Alt*], almost to the extent of confounding itself with the sense impression [*forvexler sig selv med Sandse-Indtrykket*]. In comparison with the child, the youth is more turned inward, but in imagination; he dreams, or it is as though everything about him were dreaming. (1962a:113)

At the initial stage of Kierkegaard's dialectic, there is no differentiation between the self and its social and natural world. Completely dominated by sensuous inclination and lacking any clear self-consciousness, the child "dreams itself sensuously at one with everything." This identification of self and other begins to break down with the acquisition of cognitive capacities. Stated concisely, "reflection is the negation of immediacy" (1962b:73). Kierkegaard explains this process in more detail when he writes:

> That which annuls immediacy, therefore is language [*Sproget*]. If man could not speak then he would remain in immediacy. J. C. [Johannes Climacus] thought that this might be expressed by saying that immediacy therefore is reality and language is ideality. . . . Reality I cannot express in language, for to indicate it, I must use ideality, which is a contradiction, an untruth. But how is immediacy annulled? By mediacy, which annuls immediacy by presupposing it. What, then, is immediacy? It is reality. What is mediacy? It is the word. How does the word annul actuality? By talking about it. For that which is talked about is always *presupposed*. Immediacy is reality. Language is ideality. (1967:148–49)

With the development of cognition and linguistic facility, consciousness and self-consciousness emerge. The individual is able to identify determinate objects in the field of sensual flux, to distinguish subjectivity and objectivity, and to differentiate himself from himself in the act of self-reflection. In other words, at the reflective pole of the aesthetic stage, there is a fundamental bifurcation of self and other, and of self from itself. Having differentiated subject and object, and having distinguished ideality from reality within oneself, free purposeful activity becomes possible for the first time. Since Kierkegaard contends that decision is constitutive of individual selfhood, he argues that the self becomes actual only after passing through immediacy to reflection. But a person can remain at the reflective aesthetic stage. In this case, life becomes the kind of fantastic imagination existence depicted in Schlegel's *Lucinde* and in Kierkegaard's "Diary of a Seducer." To move beyond the sensual immediacy of imaginative reflection of aesthetic existence,/24/ it is necessary to engage the will in free decision. This thrusts one into the ethical stage.

While the primary characteristic of the aesthetic stage is the absence of the exercise of the self's freedom in choice, the fundamental feature of ethical existence is the emergence of decision. This marks a crucial phase in the process of self-differentiation and individuation. At the ethical stage, one becomes a self through decisions by which one forges a personal history. We have noted that reflection enables one to discriminate ideality and reality. With respect to the personality, reflection engenders a distinction between the real self (actuality or the is) and the ideal self (possibility or the ought). Self-fulfillment then requires the effort to realize the ideal, to actualize the possible, or to mediate the ought and the is through free resolution. Reflecting the significant influence Kant exercised on his thought, Kierkegaard argues that ethical ideality always expresses itself in terms of universality.

> The ethical as such is the universal, and as the universal it applies to everyone, which may be expressed from another point of view by saying that it applies every instant. . . . Conceived immediately as physical and psychical,

> the particular individual is the individual who has his *telos* in the universal, and his ethical task is to express himself constantly in it, to abolish his particularity in order to become the universal. . . . Whenever the individual after he has entered the universal feels an impulse to assert himself as the particular, he is in temptation, and he can labor himself out of this only by penitently abandoning himself as the particular in the universal. (1970:64–65)

For the ethicist, authenticity involves the struggle to embody universal moral laws in concrete individual existence.

Kierkegaard, like Hegel, is unwilling to identify Kantian moralism with fully realized selfhood. As we have pointed out, the ethical stage is a clear advance over aesthetic existence. The ethicist differentiates himself from his social and natural matrix and constitutes his own identity by decisions in which he both seeks to control natural inclination and attempts to establish moral relations with other independent persons. Nevertheless Kierkegaard insists that complete individuality lies beyond the ethical domain. In the first place, the ethicist has no clear sense of his existence over against God. At this stage, the divine and the ethical are completely identified. For Kierkegaard, this is tantamount to a denial of the divine. Whereas Hegel criticizes the Kantian position for remaining too heteronomous, for Kierkegaard ethical existence is not heteronomous enough.

> The ethical is the universal, and as such it is again the divine. One has therefore a right to say that fundamentally every duty is a duty toward God; but if one cannot say more, then one affirms at the same time that properly I have no duty toward God. . . . Thus it is a duty to love one's neighbor, but in performing this duty I do not come into relation with God but with the neighbor whom I love. If I say then in this connection that it is my duty to love God, I am really uttering only a tautology, inasmuch as 'God' is in this instance used in an entirely abstract sense as the divine, i.e., the universal, i.e., duty. So the whole existence of the human race is rounded off completely like a sphere, and the ethical is at once its limit and its content. God becomes an invisible vanishing point, a powerless thought, His power being only in the ethical which is the content of existence. (1970:78)

Since authentic selfhood requires a clear recognition of the otherness of God and the dependence of self, ethical existence can only be an intermediate stage on life's way. In the second place, Kierkegaard maintains that individuality can never reach fulfillment in universal determinations. In a passage that at once criticizes the ethicist and points toward the final stage in this dialectical progression, Kierkegaard writes:

> Faith is precisely this paradox, that the individual as the individual is higher than the universal, is justified over against it, is not subordinate but superior— yet in such a way, be it observed, that it is the individual who, after he has been subordinated as the individual to the universal, now through the universal becomes the individual who as the individual is superior to the universal, for the fact that the individual as the individual stands in an absolute relation to the absolute. (1970:66)/25/

This is a concise description of the faithful solitude ideally embodied in Abraham./26/

Kierkegaard's Abraham is a faithful wanderer. In a characteristic text, Kierkegaard maintains: faith "does not join men together—no, it separates them—in order to unite every single individual with God. And when a person has become such that he can belong to God, he has died away from that which joins men." (1967b:no. 2052). Since "intercourse with God is in the deepest sense and absolutely non-social" (1962a:334), Abraham had to journey to Moriah alone. Sarah was left behind, and though Isaac accompanied his father, neither communication nor communion was possible for them. Faithful solitude is always shrouded in silence. Only by separating himself from all other persons could Abraham come into absolute relation to the absolute.

The God Abraham encountered during his lonely journey is not immanent in the social or natural process, but is wholly other, the transcendent Lord and governor upon whom the created order is fully dependent. In relation to such a God, there is but one proper stance: absolute obedience. Kierkegaard makes this point in terms previously noted.

> The paradox can also be expressed by saying that there is an absolute duty toward God; for in this relationship of duty the individual as an individual stands related absolutely to the absolute . . . . If this duty is absolute, the ethical is reduced to a position of relativity. (1970:80)

This paradoxical situation is the heart of Kierkegaard's analysis of Abraham. Abraham believed that God had commanded him to sacrifice his only son, Isaac. Unlike a tragic hero such as Agamemnon, this deed did not represent a higher form of ethical responsibility. To the contrary, Abraham's sacrifice of Isaac had nothing to do with ethics; it was counter to moral law—a teleological suspension of the ethical. The demand to slay his son was a test of Abraham's faith in God. Of course, this does not mean that the religious stage abolishes ethical requirements. As we have stressed, each stage preserves, though relativizes, the earlier stage(s). Ethically speaking, Abraham's duty to love his son remained binding, even though it was contravened by the higher obligation to God. It is precisely this tension that gave rise to the fear and trembling in Abraham's situation. In light of Kierkegaard's view of the relationship among the stages, we must conclude that the first stage also persists in religious existence. Abraham continued to have deep and sincere affection for Isaac. Not only did Abraham's faith lead him to suspend the ethical, it also completely contradicted his feelings. Rather than reconciling self with other and integrating obligation and inclination, Abraham's relation to God isolated him from other selves and created a painful opposition between desire and duty. Abraham's willingness to capitulate to the unreasonable divine dictate was the act of faith in which his individual selfhood reached its fullest expression.

It should be clear that beneath their contrasting evaluations of Abraham, there is substantial agreement between the views of the nature of Abrahamic faith developed by Hegel and Kierkegaard. Both believe Abraham to embody a form of life in which selfhood comes to completion in isolation from other persons and in perfect servitude to a transcendent Lord. Moreover, it would seem that Kierkegaard would agree with Hegel's claim that the positive relation to the divine for which Abraham longed could be established only by unqualified obedience to God expressed in a completely negative relation to the world and the self. But this is an oversimplification, for precisely at this point an important difference between the interpretations of Abraham developed by Kierkegaard and Hegel emerges. Throughout *Fear and Trembling*, Kierkegaard consistently describes faith as a double movement comprised of a negative and a positive moment. He calls the negative moment "infinite resignation," by which the individual relinquishes the entire sphere of finitude in an act of devout obedience to the transcendent God. Knights of infinite resignation are "strangers in the world" who "find joy and repose in pain" (1970:52, 60).

> In infinite resignation there is a peace and rest; every man . . . can train himself to make this movement which in its pain reconciles one with existence. Infinite resignation is that shirt we read about in the old fable. The thread is spun under tears, the cloth bleached with tears, the shirt sewn with tears; but then too it is a better protection than iron and steel. The imperfection in the fable is that a third party can manufacture this shirt. The secret in life is that everyone must sew it for himself, and the astonishing thing is that a man can sew it fully as well as a woman. In the infinite resignation there is peace and rest and comfort in sorrow—that is, if the movement is made normally. (1970:56)

From Kierkegaard's perspective, this is the final movement made by Hegel's Abraham.

But, Kierkegaard argues, "infinite resignation is the last stage prior to faith so that one who has not made this movement has not faith" (1970:57). In other words, Hegel's Abraham falls short of faith in *sensu eminentiori*. Kierkegaard explains:

> By faith I made renunciation of nothing, on the contrary, by faith I acquire everything, precisely in the sense in which it is said that he who has faith like a grain of mustard can remove mountains. A purely human courage is required to renounce the whole of the temporal to gain the eternal. . . . But a paradoxical and humble courage is required to grasp the whole of the temporal by virtue of the absurd, and this is the courage of faith. By faith Abraham did not renounce his claim upon Isaac, but by faith he got Isaac. (1970:59)

After having made the movement of resignation in which he willingly sacrificed his son, Abraham made the movement of faith in which he believingly received Isaac again from the hand of the Lord. Faith is the absurdly paradoxical act of simultaneously resigning and appropriating, negating and affirming, the created order. As Kierkegaard points out, "this sort of possessing is at the same time a relinquishing" (1970:57). Hence unlike the knight of infinite resignation and Hegel's Abraham, the knight of faith is no stranger in the world, but lives fully in the finite.

> And yet, and yet the whole earthly form he exhibits is a new creation by virtue of the absurd. He resigned everything infinitely, and then he grasped everything again by virtue of the absurd. He constantly makes the movements of infinity, but he does this with such correctness and assurance that he constantly gets the finite out of it, and there is not a second when one has a notion of anything else. . . . Most people live dejectedly in worldly sorrow and joy; they are the ones who sit along the wall and do not join in the dance. The knights of infinity are dancers and possess elevation. They make the movements upward, and fall down again; and this too is no mean pastime, nor ungraceful to behold. But whenever they fall down they are not able at once to assume the posture, they vacillate an instant, and this vacillation shows that after all they are strangers in the world. . . . But to be able to fall down in such a way that the same second it looks as if one were standing and walking, to transform the leap of life into a walk, absolutely to express the sublime in the pedestrian—that only the knight of faith can do—and this is the one and only prodigy. (1970:51–52)

The involvement of the knight of faith in the finite world always remains paradoxical. It is not immediate, but is mediated by his relationship to the wholly other God who infinitely transcends and completely sustains his creation. The breach between the finite and the infinite leads to the omnipresent threat of a conflict between one's obligation to these two realms. This paradoxical point of ultimate tension is, for Kierkegaard, the frontier of authentic selfhood. In the face of an all-powerful Master, the individual recognizes his finitude and becomes aware of his profound responsibility for himself. Paradoxically, freedom lies in freely appropriated bondage, and bondage is the misguided effort to negate divine Lordship. The journey to this frontier must be undertaken alone, for "in these regions partnership is unthinkable" (1970:82). As Kierkegaard concludes elsewhere, "The Christian combat is always waged by the individual; for this precisely is spirit, that everyone is an individual before God, that 'fellowship' is a lower category than 'the single individual,' which everyone can and should be" (1967c:218).

V. Phenomenologies of Spirit

Throughout their extended philosophical and theological writings, Hegel and Kierkegaard attempt to develop phenomenologies of spirit which seek to lead the reader from inauthentic to authentic or fully realized selfhood. Although the destinations of their alternative journeys differ significantly, the courses they chart bear remarkable similarities to each other. Hegel's dialectic moves from the harmonious nondifferentiation of self and other, through the

negation of this primordial unification in which opposition and estrangement
arise, to the negation of this negative moment in which there is a reintegration
or reconciliation of self and other. The Kierkegaardian dialectic of selfhood
describes a gradual process of individualization by means of the negation of
the undifferentiated identity of self and other, and the affirmation of individual selfhood in contrast with or in opposition to otherness. By focusing on their
interpretations of Abraham, we have been able to establish a dialogue between
Hegel and Kierkegaard in which the complexity of their dialectical relationship to one another has begun to emerge. We have discovered that what Hegel
regards as self-realization Kierkegaard sees as self-alienation, and what Hegel
interprets as self-estrangement is for Kierkegaard self-fulfillment. Conversely,
what Kierkegaard views as authentic selfhood, Hegel believes to be
inauthentic selfhood, and what Kierkegaard sees as inauthenticity is for Hegel
authenticity. Consequently while Hegel argues that Abraham's faith represents the extreme of alienation negated in the reconciliation revealed by Jesus,
Kierkegaard insists that Abraham's faithful solitude is the complete actualization of individual selfhood. The journey to Moriah leads in different directions.

Notes

/1/   See, e.g., Niels Thulstrup, *Kierkegaards forhold til Hegel og til den
spekulative idealisme intil 1846* (København: Gyldendahl, 1967), and William J.
Brazill, *The Young Hegelians* (New Haven: Yale University, 1970).

/2/   I have examined the coherence of Kierkegaard's writings in *Kierkegaard's
Pseudonymous Authorship: A Study of Time and the Self.*

/3/   This similarity is all the more remarkable when one realizes that these writings
were not published until this century. Hence there would seem to be little likelihood of
any direct influence of Hegel's analysis of Abraham on Kierkegaard's discussion. See
Hegels Theologische Jugendschriften, ed. Herman Nohl (Tübingen: Mohr, 1907).

/4/   As Harris points out, this work grew out of a series of shorter essays Hegel
had been preparing throughout 1798 and 1799 (330). Unlike Harris, however, I
believe "The Spirit of Christianity and Its Fate" represents a decisive turning point in
Hegel's development. In following this line of argument, I side with Professor Dieter
Henrich against Harris. See: Harris, 294–95n, and Henrich, 9–40.

/5/   For details of Hegel's relation to romanticism, see Henrich, and Taylor,
1977:95–116.

/6/   Harris has carefully documented Hegel's preoccupation with the figure of
Abraham throughout this period. The materials finally included in "The Spirit of
Christianity and Its Fate" are abstracted from numerous drafts on Abraham written
between 1797 and 1799. Harris, 27ff.

/7/   It should be noted that Hegel's view of Judaism does not change significantly
throughout his career.

/8/   Hegel's argument at this point is a remarkable anticipation of Feuerbach's analysis of the origin and the function of religion developed in *Lectures on the Essence of Religion* and of Freud's position in *The Future of an Illusion*. See *Lectures on the Essence of Religion*, trans. Ralph Manheim (New York: Harper & Row, 1967), pp. 131, 250–54; *The Future of an Illusion*, trans. W. D. Robson-Scott (New York: Doubleday, 1964), pp. 21–28.

/9/   It should be evident that the essential features of Hegel's famous analysis of the master-slave dialectic developed in the *Phänomenologie des Geistes* are already present in his discussion of the God-self relation. What we do not see at this stage in his thought is the dialectical reversal by which the slave becomes the master and the master becomes the slave.

/10/   In Hegel's later writings, the oppositional quality of Abraham's faith is incorporated in his interpretation of *Verstand*. According to the principles of understanding, "the determinations of thought are absolutely exclusive and different and remain unalterably independent in relation to each other" (1968:18–19).

/11/   As we shall see in what follows, Abraham's exclusive relation to God is the source of further opposition.

/12/   I use the word "devotion" in this context to call attention to the parallel between Hegel's analysis of Abraham and his discussion of the "unhappy consciousness" in the *Phenomenology*. In the later work, devotion (*Andacht*) is one of the fundamental ways in which the believer approaches God. The term suggests the servility of the relationship.

/13/   The abstract otherness of God and the quantitative infinity of divine demands are definitive characteristics of what Hegel later labels the "bad infinite." See: 1969, 139–43.

/14/   This way of stating the argument points toward the complex epistemological analyses developed in Hegel's mature system. The attempt to reconcile self and world, self and God, and self and self, is nothing more than the effort to establish absolute knowledge.

/15/   And, we might add, of Enlightenment philosophy in general, and Kantian philosophy in particular.

/16/   In fact, Hegel sometimes sounds like a Marcionite.

/17/   This text is an explicit anticipation of Hegel's mature position. In his completed system, spirit and reason play a role strictly parallel to the notion of love in the early writings. The *telos* of Hegel's entire philosophical endeavor is precisely the reconciliation prefigured in the analysis of love.

/18/   Quoted by Harris, 316n.

/19/   Throughout this section of the discussion, we have stressed the way in which Hegel's analysis of love foreshadows central aspects of his developed system. One significant difference should be noted. At this stage, Hegel does not think that the unity apprehended in love can be grasped through rational reflection. To the contrary, reflection ruptures the harmonious unity established in love. "The connection of infinite and finite is of course a 'holy mystery,' because this connection is life itself. Reflective thinking which partitions life, can distinguish it into infinite and finite, and then it is only the restriction, the finite regarded by itself, which affords the concept of man as opposed to the divine. But outside reflective thinking, and in truth, there is no such restriction" (1971:262). Clearly, Hegel's position on the role of reason in the achievement of reconciliation changes radically. As we have suggested, reason later fulfills the function previously accomplished by love.

/20/   In some contexts, Kierkegaard presents refinements of this threefold scheme. For our purposes, however, the triadic structure is most important.

/21/   In their eagerness to delineate the differences separating Hegel and Kierkegaard, most commentators overlook the no less significant positive relation between their positions. This essay as a whole attempts to underscore the necessity to reconsider the Hegel-Kierkegaard relationship.

/22/   Hegel, of course, does not use biological language to make this point.

/23/   In order to evaluate Kierkegaard's critique of the Hegelian system, it is essential to stress that Hegel insists that difference remains in the final unification. In terms of selfhood, the reconciliation of self with other enhances and does not abrogate individuality. From the perspective of Kierkegaard's criticism, the third moment of Hegel's dialectic is a simple reversion to the first moment. Our discussion has made it clear that this is contrary to Hegel's intention. Existentialist critics of Hegel have been too willing to accept Kierkegaard's misrepresentation of the Hegelian position.

/24/   Developing the Hegelian notion of *aufheben*, Kierkegaard argues that each earlier stage is taken up into (*ophaeve*) the later stage(s) in such a way that it is simultaneously displaced and preserved.

/25/   Lowrie obscures this important passage by translating *Enkelte* as "particular" rather than as "individual."

/26/   Kant himself commented on the Abraham story: "Abraham would have had to answer this supposedly divine voice: 'That I ought to kill my good son, that is wholly certain; but that you, who appear to me, are God, of that I am not certain and never can become certain, even if it should resound from the (visible) heavens.'" *Friedens-Abschluss und Beilegung des Streits der Fakulten*, quoted by Walter Kaufmann in *Hegel: Reinterpretation, Texts, and Commentary* (New York: Doubleday, 1965), p. 271.

Works Consulted

Crites, Stephen
    1961   *The Problem of the "Positivity" of the Gospel in Hegel's Dialectic of Alienation and Reconciliation.* Ph.D. dissertation. Yale University.

Harris, H. S.
    1972   *Hegel's Development Toward The Sunlight, 1770–1801.* Oxford: Clarendon Press.

Hegel, G. W. F.
    1967   *Phenomenology of Mind.* Trans. J. B. Baillie. New York: Harper & Row.
    1968   *Lectures on the Philosophy of Religion.* Trans. E. B. Spiers and J. B Sanderson. New York: Humanities Press.
    1969   *Science of Logic.* Trans. A.V. Miller. New York: Humanities Press.
    1971   *Early Theological Writings.* Trans. T. M. Knox. Philadelphia: University of Pennsylvania Press.

Henrich, Dieter
    1971   *Hegel im Kontext.* Frankfurt: Suhrkamp.

Hyppolite, Jean
    1974   *Genesis and Structure of Hegel's Phenomenology of Spirit.* Trans. S. Cherniak and J. Heckman. Evanston: Northwestern University Press.

Kaufmann, Walter
    1965   *Hegel: Reinterpretation, Texts, and Commentary.* New York: Doubleday.

Kierkegaard, Søren
    1962a   *Christian Discourses.* Trans. W. Lowrie. New York: Oxford University Press.
    1962b   *The Point of View of My Work as an Author: A Report to History.* Trans. W. Lowrie. New York: Harper & Row.
    1967a   *De Omnibus Dubitandum Est.* Trans. T. H. Croxall. Stanford: Stanford University Press.
    1967b   *Journals and Papers.* Trans. Howard and Edna Hong. Bloomington: Indiana University Press.
    1967c   *Training in Christianity.* Trans. W. Lowrie. Princeton: Princeton University Press.
    1970   *Fear and Trembling.* Trans. W. Lowrie. Princeton: Princeton University Press.

Marx, Karl
    1967   *Writings of the Young Marx on Philosophy and Society.* Trans. L. D. Easton and K. H. Guddat. New York: Doubleday.

Taylor, Mark C.
    1975   *Kierkegaard's Pseudonymous Authorship: A Study of Time
                    and the Self.* Princeton: Princeton University Press.
    1977   "Love and Forms of Spirit: Hegel vs. Kierkegaard," *Kierke-
                    gaardiana.* Volume 10.

Itinerarium Mentis in Deum:
Hegel's Proofs of God's Existence

I. Proofs of God's Existence

Paul Tillich begins one of his most suggestive essays by characterizing what he regards as "the two types of philosophy of religion."

> One can distinguish two ways of approaching God: the way of overcoming estrangement and the way of meeting a stranger. In the first way man discovers himself when he discovers God; it transcends him infinitely, something from which he is estranged, but from which he never has been and never can be separated. In the second way man meets a *stranger* when he meets God. The meeting is accidental. Essentially they do not belong to each other. They may become friends on a tentative and conjectural basis. But there is no certainty about the stranger man has met. (10)

The former approach to God Tillich calls ontological, the latter he labels cosmological. Tillich maintains that these two types of the philosophy of religion stand in tension throughout the Christian tradition. From the cosmological perspective, the approach to God is indirect and inferential. What knowledge of God we are able to attain through reason is based upon or inferred from experience in the world—it is a *demonstrationes ex finito*. Beginning with an examination of finite sense data, one argues to God as the infinite and necessary explanatory ground of the experienced world. Rather than bringing the infinite and the finite closer together, this line of reasoning reveals the abyss separating the creative God and the created world. God remains a stranger—known, but dimly from afar. According to the ontological argument, knowledge of God is not the conclusion of an inferential process, but is the necessary presupposition of any intellectual inquiry. God is regarded as truth itself; *Veritas est Deus—Deus est Veritas*. The quest for truth presupposes an implicit awareness of God that becomes explicit with the attainment of knowledge. To the extent that one knows the true (the good, or the beautiful), the divine *Logos* indwells the human *logos*. God is not an alien Wholly Other, a stranger, but is immanent in, though transcendent, to the self. The exploration of the rational foundation of truth discloses the inseparability of subjectivity and objectivity, thought and being, God and self (or God and world). There need be no inference from one to the other, for they mutually inhere as ground and fulfillment of each other. Knowledge of God negates estrangement and brings reconciliation with essential being.

During the early years of the Enlightenment, these two approaches to the knowledge of God enjoyed considerable support among many philosophers and theologians. Following the lead of thinkers such as Descartes, Leibniz, and Wolff, continental rationalists formulated variations of the ontological argument, while their more empirically minded British counterparts such as Collins, Toland, and Paley elaborated different forms of the cosmological and teleological arguments. But the situation changed significantly in the latter half of the eighteenth century. Hume's posthumous *Dialogues Concerning Natural Religion* (1777) and Kant's First Critique (1781) called into question the entire enterprise of proving God's existence on theoretical grounds. After the devastating criticisms of Hume and Kant, there seemed to be only two possibilities. Either one could side with Hume, confessing man's inability to prove God's existence and declaring an "honest" skepticism in matters theological or one could join Kant in seeking to reestablish the certainty of the existence of the divine on other than theoretical grounds.

As was his wont, Hegel rejected both of these alternatives. Although acutely aware of the disrepute into which the proofs of the existence of God recently had fallen, Hegel undertook their reexamination with the expressed intention of restoring them to philosophical and theological respectability. As Hegel's argument unfolds, it becomes apparent that his interpretation of the nature and function of the proofs plays an important role in his overall philosophical undertaking. By recapitulating the movements exhibited by the proofs, Hegel's system results in a single complex proof of God's existence. To see precisely how this is so is the task before us in the following pages.

II. Proofs as Proof

Hegel notes that historically there have been three fundamental forms of the proof of God's existence: the cosmological, the teleological, and the ontological arguments. In agreement with Tillich, Hegel holds that these three arguments fall into two general categories, depicting different dimensions of the relation between God and the world, or between the infinite and the finite. On the one hand, the cosmological and teleological arguments start from experience in the world and seek God as its ground or necessary cause. The ontological approach, on the other hand, begins with the notion of God and tries to establish God's being and the actuality of the world. But while Tillich seems to suggest an either-or between the cosmological/teleological and the ontological arguments, Hegel insists that an adequate analysis of the proofs of God's existence must include the valid features of *both* approaches. Such an integration of the proofs is possible only if they are recast in the mold of speculative philosophy. The development of an acceptable interpretation of the proofs depends upon an advance beyond the viewpoint of analytic understanding (*Verstand*) to the perspective of dialectical reason (*Vernunft*).

Elaborating a distinction identified by Kant,/1/ Hegel describes understanding as the capacity to analyze extant things into discrete parts and to identify specific differences definitive of isolated entities. The guiding rules of analytic understanding are abstract self-identity and the law of non-contradiction, according to which "the determinations of thought are absolutely exclusive and different, and remain unalterably independent in relation to each other" (1968a:III, 18–19). Hegel summarizes his point when he writes: "Thought, as *understanding*, sticks to fixed determinations and to the distinction of one thing from another: every such limited abstract it treats as having a subsistence of its own" (1968b:par. 80). When Hegel turns his attention to the manner of demonstration characteristic of analytic understanding, the importance of his view of this type of reflection for his interpretation of the proofs of God's existence emerges. An analytical argument begins with a fixed presupposition from which it seeks to draw a definite conclusion. Since this form of thought is governed by the principles of abstract self-identity and non-contradiction, the starting point and the conclusion retain their isolated independence and the relationship between them is external. The problem, then, is to bridge the gap between the presupposition and the conclusion which is created by analysis itself. In the particular instance of the proofs of God's existence, understanding attempts to argue from contingent to necessary being, from finite to infinite design, or from the thought of God to the being of God. According to Hegel, all previous proofs were variations of this type of argumentation. This is the source of their fundamental deficiency and the ground of their inevitable shortcoming. What analytic understanding so sharply separates, it cannot effectively reunite—its arguments are sophistic. The abyss between the defined oppositions remains so wide that it can be crossed only by a blind leap of faith. Hegel concludes that Kant's criticisms of the effort of understanding to prove God's existence are persuasive. Contrary to Kant, however, Hegel does not believe that the inability of analytic understanding to fashion an adequate theoretical proof of God's existence implies the impossibility of this task. In fact, dialectical reason accomplishes what analytic understanding fails to achieve.

Instead of analyzing and separating into discrete parts, dialectical reason synthesizes and integrates into internally differentiated wholes that simultaneously maintain the differences identified, but incorrectly interpreted, by analytic understanding. From the point of view of reason, everything concrete is a union of conflicting tendencies. Opposites are not mutually exclusive, but coinhere and necessarily entail one another; each is what it is through its own other. The identity of a specific entity is a function of the relation to, rather than the abstraction or the isolation from, its opposite. Since relations are internal and necessary and not external and supplementary, every concrete actuality includes *in its own self* its other as definitive and constitutive of itself. Therefore the examination of any particularity inevitably leads to its contrary, through which it establishes its concrete identity. It should be apparent that dialectical reason abrogates the basic principles of analytic understanding—abstract identity and non-contradiction. The hard-and-fast distinctions of understanding are abstractions from the contradictions inherently characteristic of determinate reality, and negate themselves when submitted to rational reflection. This is not to suggest that reason abolishes distinctions. To the contrary, it "is just this act of distinguishing or differentiating which at the same time gives no difference and does not hold this difference as permanent" (1968a:III, 18). For dialectical reason, the move from contingency to necessity, from finite to infinite design, or from thought to being, does not require a leap or an arbitrary transition between exclusive opposites. Having ascertained the relational character of concrete identity, dialectical reason recognizes that each member of the opposition necessarily entails the other. Rational argumentation involves the explication of the implicit or immanent relation by the means of which opposites maintain themselves in their concretion. Hegel argues that dialectical reason creates the possibility of an interpretation of the proofs of God's existence which meets the criticisms to which they recently had been subjected.

Before considering the individual proofs, however, we must return to the problem of Hegel's general view of their nature and function. Hegel insists that the three proofs of God's existence are not separate arguments, but are dialectical moments of a single complex proof. The rational (as well as the historical) order of the proofs is: cosmological, teleological, ontological. Each later proof passes beyond, while at the same time assuming and preserving, its predecessor(s). Once we recognize the dialectic of these three moments of the argument for God's existence, we are in a position to glimpse the relationship of the argument to Hegel's entire philosophy of religion and to his system as a whole. Each proof is the correlate of a different stage of the philosophy of religion: the cosmological proof corresponds to the religion of nature; the teleological proof corresponds to the religion of spiritual individuality, and the ontological proof corresponds to the absolute religion.

In addition to this, Hegel's interpretation of the relationship between religious imagination and speculative philosophy suggests further implications of the proofs of God's existence. According to Hegel, the exercise of religious imagination issues in representations, *Vorstellungen*, that point toward, but finally fail to express, the universality of philosophical thought. Speculative philosophy seeks to articulate the conceptual content represented in religious images. Through rational reflection, religious *Vorstellungen* are rendered philosophical *Begriffe*. Hegel insists that the distinction between *Vorstellung* and *Begriff* is formal, rather than substantive.

> Philosophy thus characterizes itself as a cognition [*Erkennen*] of the necessity in the content of the absolute representation [*Vorstellung*] . . . This cognition is thus the *recognition* [*Anerkenne*] of this content and its form; it is the

> release from the one-sidedness of the forms, raising them into the absolute
> form, which determines itself to content, remains identical with it, and is in
> that the cognition of that essential and actual necessity. This movement,
> which philosophy is, finds itself already accomplished, when at the close it
> grasps its own notion [*Begriff*]—i.e., only reflects on its knowledge. (1968b:par.
> 573)

From this perspective, the translation process underlying the philosophical
enterprise results in the sublation (rather than the simple negation) of
Vorstellung in *Begriff*. By viewing the relation of religious imagination and
speculative reason in these terms, Hegel is able to suggest another significant
connection between the proofs of God's existence and his overall philosophical system. He maintains that the three moments of the proof *represent* the
conceptual progress reflected in the *Logic*. Logic's movement from the doctrine of being, defined as determinate being (*Dasein*), to the doctrine of
essence recapitulates the advance from contingency to necessity developed
in the cosmological argument. Hegel characterizes necessity in the first proof
alternatively as essence, cause, ground, substance, and force, all variations of
the logical doctrine of essence. Through the concept of determination in
accordance with an end, the teleological argument defines more concretely
the absolute necessity of the cosmological proof. The transition from the
cosmological to the teleological argument is paralleled by the logical move
from the doctrine of essence to the doctrine of the notion (*Der Begriff*).
Specifically, the consideration of the teleological determination of the object
elucidates those aspects of rational cognition defined in the teleological argument. As the ontological argument realizes the truth implicit in the cosmological and teleological arguments by disclosing the identity of being and
thought, so the absolute idea reconciles being and essence, thereby revealing
Veritas Ipsa, or God. Finally in more comprehensive terms, Hegel's whole
philosophical system forms an intricate argument for God's existence. While
the transition from logic to the philosophy of nature and of spirit is the
ontological moment of Hegel's proof, the movement from the philosophy of
nature and of spirit to absolute knowledge or to speculative philosophy is the
cosmological/teleological moment of his argument.

When Hegel's threefold proof of God's existence is placed within the
context of his complete system, it becomes evident that this argument charts
the course of the mind from sensible intuition to truth, or from immediate
experience in the world to God. The proof is the *Itinerarium Mentis in
Deum*. Hegel is suggesting that "what men call the proofs of God's existence
are, rightly understood, ways of describing and analyzing the native course
of the mind, the course of *thought* thinking the *data* of the senses. The rise
of thought above the world of sense, its passage from the finite to the
infinite . . . is thought and nothing but thought" (1968b:par. 80). This insight
should not obscure the two rhythms of the single proof that we have
identified: the cosmological/teleological—from finitude to infinity; and the

ontological—from infinity to finitude. In tracing the *Itinerarium Mentis in Deum*, the cosmological and teleological moments of the proof presuppose the *Descensus Dei im Mundum* described in the ontological argument. In other words, the cosmological and teleological moments of the proof are incomplete and incorrect without the ontological moment./2/ Human ascent retraces divine descent—apart from creation and incarnation, there can be no resurrection and salvation.

III. The Cosmological Argument

Historically and philosophically, the first form of the proof of God's existence is *ex contingentia mundi*. As we have noted, earlier expressions of the cosmological argument are guided by analytic understanding and rest upon the fundamental tenet of abstract self-identity, according to which contingency and necessity (or finitude and infinitude)/3/ are defined as mutually exclusive opposites. The world as immediately experienced is identified as manifold, contingent, and finite, while God is construed as one, absolutely necessary, and infinite. The "proof" consists of arguing from the world to God, the world's necessary cause or explanatory ground. Stated concisely: "*Because* . . . the contingent, is, or exists, *therefore* . . . the absolutely necessary, is or exists" (1968a:III, 281)./4/ Hegel contends that so conceived, the cosmological argument inverts the proper relation between the contingent/finite and the absolutely necessary/infinite, hence demonstrating the converse of what it sets out to prove. If one follows analytic understanding, one is led to conclude that "contingent things condition absolute necessity . . . and thus necessity appears as if it were something whose existence is presupposed as dependent on or conditioned by contingent things. Absolute necessity is in this way put in a position of dependence, so that contingent things remain outside of it" (1968a:II, 145–46). In short, the contingent seems self-subsistent and necessary, and the necessary appears dependent and contingent. Moreover, by establishing a dualism between the finite and the infinite, the infinite is opposed to, excluded from, and limited by the finite. The result of the argument, therefore, is that the finite, *as finite*, assumes the characteristics of infinity, and infinity is finitized.

Hegel believes that the form of the cosmological argument developed by dialectical reason overcomes the obvious errors of analytic understanding's version of the proof. Beginning with a reexamination of finitude and contingency, dialectical reason recognizes that the finite is not independent and self-identical, but is *inherently* dependent and self-contradictory. Because the contingent/finite does not possess aseity, its being necessarily entails the being of an other, i.e., its opposite or the absolutely necessary/infinite. Apart from the infinite or absolutely necessary, the finite or contingent is not. In Hegel's form of the cosmological argument, there is no movement from independent finitude to transcendent infinity. A rational consideration of finite or contingent being discloses its dialectical, internal relation to infinity or absolute necessity. As Hegel puts it, *"The being of the finite is not only its being*, but is also the being of the infinite" (1968a:III, 254). Finitude and contingency include within themselves their opposites as indispensable presuppositions, necessary constituents, and the essential ground of their being. The determinate identity of finitude or contingency comprehends its own difference (infinitude/necessity) in such a way that the relationship to otherness is actually a dimension of self-relation requisite for self-realization. The following text at once indicates Hegel's chief criticism of analytic understanding's cosmological argument and presents his own statement of the proof.

> What the study of the finite from a speculative point of view really yields, is not merely the thought, that if the finite exists, the infinite exists too, not that being is to be defined as not merely finite, but that it is further defined as infinite. If the finite were this affirmative, the major proposition would be the proposition—finite being as finite is infinite. . . . The statement that ought to constitute the major proposition of the syllogism must rather take the following form: the being of the finite is not its own being, but is, on the contrary, the being of its other, namely the infinite. Or to put it otherwise, being which is characterized as finite possesses this characteristic only in the sense that it cannot exist independently in relation to the infinite, but is, the contrary, merely ideal—a moment of the infinite. Consequently the minor proposition: the finite *is*—disappears in any affirmative sense, and if we may still say it exists, we mean that its existence is merely an appearance or phenomenal existence. It is just the fact that the finite world is merely a manifestation or appearance that constitutes the absolute power of the infinite. (1968a:III, 260)

In this form, the cosmological argument represents the course thought follows in determining the truth of contingency or of finitude. To know the finite or contingent truly is to know it as a manifestation of the infinite or absolutely necessary. The world assumes true proportion only when it is apprehended as created by God.

Hegel's account of the cosmological argument also addresses the second major problem encountered by earlier forms of the proof—the finitization of the infinite. It will be recalled that as a result of the use of the principle of abstract identity, analytic understanding limits the infinite by the finite and makes the absolutely necessary dependent upon the contingent. But the examination of finitude by dialectical reason has shown the self-contradiction implicit in such abstract identity, and has laid bare the thoroughly relational character of concrete self-identity. The finite includes the infinite as a moment of itself. We are now in a position to see that infinity and absolute necessity, rationally comprehended, include finitude and contingency. As the finite realizes itself only in and through the infinite, so infinity constitutes itself infinite only in relation to finitude. The finite is not other than or opposed to the infinite, but is a necessary dimension of the infinite itself. To be truly infinite, the infinite must be unlimited by finitude, and must contain otherness within itself as a necessary moment of self-determination. In the very process of establishing its own self-identity, infinity sublates (*aufheben*) the otherness of its other by making finitude an essential aspect of its own being. The infinite or absolutely necessary "consists in being at home with itself in its other, or if expressed as a process, in coming to itself in its other" (1968b:par. 94). This is the true infinite, unfettered by finitude, and the genuinely absolute necessity, unconditioned by contingency.

The term Hegel uses to describe the infinite that is the process of coming to itself in its own other is "double negativity." He explains: "If we further say that the infinite is the not-finite, we have in point of fact virtually expressed its truth: for the finite itself is the first negative, the non-finite is the negative of that negation, the negation which is identical with itself and thus at the same time a true affirmation" (1968b:par. 94). Lacking self-subsistence and depending upon its other for its being, finitude is not infinite; it is the negation of infinity. Conversely, the infinite is the independent ground or necessary cause that is the negation of the finite. The analysis of the complex relation between infinity and finitude leads Hegel to conclude that since the finite is the negation of the infinite, and the infinite is the negation of the finite, the infinite actually is the negation of its own negation, or is double negativity. The infinite is that reality whose otherness is not merely other, but is a reflection of itself, that reality which comes to *itself* in its other. In Hegel's own terms: double negativity is thoroughly self-referential./5/ The infinite or absolutely necessary "is the negation of the negation—the negation relating itself to itself—and this is absolute affirmation, and is at the same time being, i.e., simple reference to itself" (1968a:I, 327–28). The infinite *is* the in-finite. It constitutes itself truly infinite by relation to and comprehension of the finite whose ground it is. If we recall Hegel's distinction between *Vorstellung* and *Begriff*, we can express the import of his philosophical version of the cosmological argument in traditional religious imagery: God assumes true proportion only when apprehended as Creator of the world.

Creator and creature, God and world, infinite and finite, necessary and contingent, bound in a thoroughly dialectical relation through which each relatum realizes itself—this is the conclusion of Hegel's speculative rendering of the cosmological argument. At this stage of reflection, however, there remains a certain specious asymmetry within the relationship. The configuration of the relation is such that the determinate identity of the former member is construed as ground or the cause of the latter, and the latter is identified primarily by being grounded in or caused by the former. In other words, God is essentially Creator, the world essentially created. The cosmological argument seeks to demonstrate that "there is only one being, and this belongs to necessity, and other things by their very nature form a part of it" (1968a:III, 315). Whereas philosophers and theologians have used categories as various as ideal, essence, ground, whole, substance, and cause to express this insight, Hegel maintains that the fundamental characteristic of the divine to emerge from the cosmological argument is more effectively captured by the terms "Power or force" (1968a:III, 328). God is the infinite power that creates and sustains all things. However, from Hegel's point of view, the conclusion of this argument is incomplete and "is not adequate to express our idea of God" (1968a:III, 313). Although the divine is recognized as the absolute, self-determining power of the world, the infinite's self-determination is abstract, its power blind. The other two moments of the proof of God's existence are necessary for a complete notion of the divine.

IV. The Teleological Argument

While the cosmological proof establishes God's power, the teleological argument reveals divine wisdom. God no longer is viewed as abstract self-determination or blind power, but is known as purposive activity—the process of determination in accordance with an end. We have noted that Hegel believes the cosmological and teleological moments of the proof to share a common rhythm: they both move from the world (effect) to God (cause). However the world that forms this common point of departure is characterized differently in the two proofs. Consequently distinguishable, though complementary notions of God result. The teleological argument takes up within itself the notion of God derived from the cosmological moment of the proof, and gives it a richer, more complete determination. God remains powerful, but now is known to exercise power wisely.

Throughout the history of theology and philosophy, however, the teleological argument also has been formulated according to the principles of analytic understanding. Instead of starting with the world viewed as an aggregate of contingent and finite entities and moving to God interpreted as infinite and necessary causal power as does the cosmological argument, the teleological argument proceeds from the relationship of means and end found in the world of common experience to God, graspsed as first cause or absolute ground of such ordered relations. In this form of the teleological argument, God is represented as a transcendent architect or infinite designer who imposes his purposes upon the world from without. The world is the means to God's end. Hegel points out that understanding again follows the pattern of analysis established in the cosmological proof. "Because there are arrangements, ends of this kind, there is a wisdom which disposes and orders everything" (1968a:III, 351). According to Hegel, this line of argument involves at least two fundamental problems. The first pertains to the character of God. Having established the relationship between God and world as mutually exclusive and external, analytic understanding is forced to conclude that God is dependent upon the world for the means by which he attempts to effect his ends. God again is pictured as conditioned, limited, and finite. In agreement with Kant, Hegel insists that such an architect should be labeled a "Demiurge," rather than God. The second problem implied in analytic understanding's version of the teleological argument concerns the character of the relationship among entities within the world. It is assumed that concrete individuals are essentially independent of one another and are related only externally or accidently. The primordial isolation of mundane entities is overcome solely through a contingent relation to an alien reality. Thus, particular individuals are not in themselves interrelated, but are merely brought together through the agency of a wholly other God who imposes extrinsic order upon the world. We might summarize both of these problems by saying that for analytic understanding, the relation of means and end is *external*, rather than internal. While God depends upon the world for the means to his end, the world depends upon God for its proper end.

Hegel believes that a reexamination of the relation between means and end through the eyes of dialectical reason opens the possibility of a satisfactory interpretation of the teleological argument. Dialectical reason defines the notion of "inner teleology"/6/ by which it sublates the apparent externality and indifference of means and end and establishes their mediated unity. Hegel argues that when means and end are rationally grasped, they are interrelated in such a way that the end has its means within itself, and the means exist as self-determinations or momentary particularizations of the end in its ongoing process of self-actualization. In contrast to the opposition of means and end in external (finite) teleology, for inner (infinite) teleology,

> the truth is in the teleological activity which is means and matter in itself, a teleological activity which accomplishes its ends through itself. This is what is meant by the infinite activity of the end. The end accomplishes itself, realizes itself through its own activity, and thus comes into harmony with itself in the process of realizing itself. The finitude of the end consists, as we saw, in the separation of means and material. . . . The truth of the determination of the end consists in the fact that the end has within itself its means, as also the material in which it realizes itself. (1968a:III, 335)

The example Hegel most frequently uses to illustrate his notion of inner teleology is the living organism. In the organism, each member is simultaneously means and end. Life is the product, the end that posits or realizes itself through organic activity. But as the organism's necessary presupposition, life is at the same time productive, i.e., the beginning. Beginning and end, producer and product are one. The living organism *is* this active self-production, or is the dynamic process of self-realization in which means and end form an inseparable dialectical relation. It should be evident, however, that while the organism, considered in itself, is a self-perpetuating totality, it remains dependent upon things outside itself. To the extent that the means of subsistence are external to the organism, we move away from inner, and toward external teleology. It might seem, therefore, that in the final analysis the organism is not illustrative of inner teleology. However, Hegel attempts to solve this dilemma by universalizing the organic metaphor. Organisms join the rest of reality to form a single totality that maintains itself through the internal differentiation and the relation of its constitutive members. "The real advance accordingly is from this finite mode of life [the living organism] to absolute, universal conformity to an end, to the thought that this world is a cosmos, a system, in which everything has an essential relation to everything else, and nothing is isolated; something which is regularly arranged in itself, in which everything has its place, is closely connected with the whole, subsists through the whole, and thus takes an active part in the production, in the life of the whole" (1968a:III, 350).

Unlike the Romantic poets from whom he learned so much, Hegel maintains that the image of the universe as one complex organism is thoroughly rational. We have seen that dialectical reason demonstrates the relational character of self-identity. Relation between self and other, or among entities, is essential (rather than accidental) to the determinate identity of any particularity. Something assumes *complete* concretion and full self-realization only through its internal relation to the whole of which it is a part. This whole, it must be emphasized, is not abstract and does not exist in isolation from its parts.

> There is nothing in the whole which is not in the parts, and nothing in the parts which is not in the whole. The whole is not abstract unity, but unity as of a diverse manifold; but this unity, as that in which the elements of the manifold are related to one another, is the determinateness of each element through which it is a part. The relation has, therefore, an inseparable identity and one self-subsistence. (1969:515–16)

Here Hegel argues that the whole is the self-identical structure of relationality that assumes concrete actuality through the particularities whose determinate identities it establishes and maintains./7/

The interpretation of the uni-verse as a single organism comprised of many cooperating organs or as an internally self-differentiated totality is especially significant for Hegel's teleological argument for God's existence. From the perspective of rational teleology, a single end is realizing itself throughout the entire cosmos. This self-realizing end is not imposed upon the world from without, but is the very life-force, soul, or subject of the world. "When we grasp this life-force in its true nature," Hegel maintains, "it is seen to be one principle, one organic life of the universe, one living system. All that is simply constitutes the organs of the one subject" (1968a:III, 343). As our analysis of Hegel's argument suggests, the activity of this "life-force" or "single subject"/8/ is governed by the principle of inner teleology. Its means are not external, but are the internal, necessary condition of the possibility of the single subject's concrete actuality. Moreover, the means (all particular entities in the world) possess their specific identity by virtue of their place within the self-realizing activity of the end. The end is no more external to the means than the means are to the end. Hegel contends that this omnipresent and perpetually active structural ground of all determinate reality is nothing other than the sovereign *Nous* or the eternal *Logos* that creates and rules the world. The speculative form of the teleological argument does not reveal the divine as an alien other who directs the world from without. According to dialectical reason, God is the immanent structural principle that sustains and directs the universe.

When the cosmos is viewed according to the principle of inner teleology, no part of the finite world can be comprehended in isolation from the self-actualizing totality of which it is an organic member. This determinate whole is the outworking or the concrete self-actualization of *Nous*. Expressed theologically, the world is the realization of God's wise purpose. "To say that the world is ruled by providence implies that design, as what has been absolutely predetermined, is the active principle, so that what becomes known corresponds to what has been foreknown and forewilled" (1968b:par. 147). The teleological argument attempts to demonstrate that "the truth of the world is the completely realized essential existence of the manifestation of a wise power" (1968a:II, 154). Through this proof, dialectical reason renders explicit the unity of subjectivity and objectivity implicit in the notion of design. In other words, the awareness of the teleological structure of reality discloses the coincidence of intention and actualization, thought and being, subjectivity and objectivity. This coincidence is truth, and truth is God.

The teleological proof, like the cosmological argument, follows the course of the mind from finite experience in the world to the rational comprehension of that experience. It charts the *Itinerarium Mentis in Deum*, the movement to *Veritas Ipsa*. The truth at the end of this journey is more complete than the truth of the cosmological argument. God, no longer regarded as simply the absolute power or force upon which all depends, is seen as wise, purposive, providential power—the *Alpha* and *Omega*. The world, no longer understood as an aggregate of contingent things, is grasped as an organically interrelated process directed toward a common end. By establishing truth as the identity of end and means, subjectivity and objectivity, or thought and being, the teleological proof identifies the structure of the Absolute Idea, whose exploration lies within the domain of the ontological argument. As the cosmological argument points to the teleological argument, so the teleological argument necessarily leads to the third moment of the proof of God's existence, the ontological argument./9/

V. The Ontological Argument

By fully realizing the truth that has been emerging in the cosmological and the teleological moments, the ontological argument is the most complete form of the proof of God's existence. This moment of the proof inversely expresses the rhythm of the cosmological/teleological approach to God. The first two proofs progress dialectically from the world to God—from determinate being to divine notion, eternal Logos, Absolute Idea. The ontological proof advances from the pure notion to its concrete existence. If the cosmological and the teleological moment is the *Itinerarium Mentis in Deum*, the ontological moment is the *Descensus Dei im Mundi*.

Hegel maintains that the overriding issue raised by the ontological argument is the problem of the relation between thought and being.

> The ontological proof starts from the notion. The notion is considered to be something subjective, and is defined as something opposed to the object and to reality. Here it constitutes the starting point, and what we have to do is to show that being, too, belongs to this notion. (1968a:III, 361)

Phrased in terms more congruent with the history of the ontological argument, starting from the idea or notion of God, an effort is made to establish the being or existence of God.

Analytic understanding is unable to grasp the ontological argument./10/ Again following the principles of abstract identity and non-contradiction, "The understanding keeps being and the notion strictly apart, and considers each as self-identical" (1968a:III, 363). Having established this gap between thought and being, subject and object, analytic understanding is unable to reunite the two./11/

Despite the protests of analytic understanding, dialectical reason insists that "the idea that being can be separated from the notion is a mere fancy." (1968a:III, 364.) In a manner analogous to the relation between finitude/infinitude, necessity/contingency, and end/means, thought and being form a dialectical unity in which the members, though distinguishable, are inseparable. Hegel's argument for the oneness of thought and being (notion and existence) falls into two major divisions. Since being can be regarded either abstractly or concretely, Hegel first seeks to demonstrate the identity of thought and pure being (*Sein*), and then attempts to establish the unity of thought and determinate being (*Dasein*). For Hegel, the successful execution of the ontological proof confirms the veracity of absolute idealism.

Hegel begins his argument by defining abstract or pure being as indeterminate, completely lacking concrete specification. Earlier stages of the proof have shown that determination (concrete self-identity) is a function of mediation with or relationship to ostensible "otherness." Indeterminate being, therefore, is immediate, un-mediated, relationless being: being that is abstracted from its relation to or mediation with otherness. In short, abstract being is simple relation-to-self. "Immediacy means in fact, being. It means this simple relation-to-self, insofar as we eliminate relation [to other]" (1968a:I, 163). Hegel holds that so conceived, being (objectivity) is one with

thought (subjectivity). "Pure being . . . is on the one hand pure thought, and
on the other hand is simple immediacy . . ." (1968b:par. 86).

To support his assertion of the identity of thought and being, Hegel
turns from an analysis of pure being to an examination of thought. He
insists, however, that thought cannot be considered apart from the thinking
subject. In this context, Hegel maintains that "thought, viewed as subject, is
what is expressed by the word I [Ich]" (1968b:par. 20). Thus, if we are to
understand thought, we must examine the nature of the I. Reflection upon
the I necessarily is reflexive. In becoming objective to itself, the I discloses its
intrinsic bifurcation or inherently self-contradictory character. The self-
conscious I is simultaneously subject and object—a self-reflexive structure in
which there is an identity of subjectivity and objectivity. Hegel elaborates
the two internally related dimensions of the I:

> But the I is, *first* this pure self-related unity, and it is so not immediately but
> only as making abstraction from all determinateness and content and with-
> drawing into the freedom of unrestricted equality with itself. As such it is
> *universality*, a unity that is unity with itself only through its *negative* atti-
> tude, which appears as a process of abstraction, and that consequently con-
> tains all determinateness dissolved in it. *Secondly*, the *I* as self-related nega-
> tivity is no less immediately *individuality*, or is *absolutely determined*, oppos-
> ing itself to all that is other and excluding it—*individual personality*. This
> absolute *universality* which is also immediately an absolute *individualization*,
> and an absolutely determined being, only through its unity with the *posited-
> ness*—this constitutes the nature of the *I* as well as of the notion; neither the
> one nor the other can be truly comprehended unless the two indicated
> moments are grasped at the same time both in their abstraction and also in
> their perfect unity. (1969: 53)/12/

Stated concisely, the self-conscious I is the *internal* dialectic of subjectivity
and objectivity./13/ Although the I's moments of subjectivity and objectivity
are inseparable and always exist in concrete unity with one another, they
can be distinguished by reflective analysis. As subject, the I is pure thought
from which all determination has been abstracted./14/ As object, the I is the
concretization of the subject—the particular form assumed by the abstract,
universal I./15/

Through the analysis of self-consciousness, it becomes evident that pure
thought, like pure being, is utterly empty, devoid of all particularity and
determination. Hegel's argument leads to the conclusion that the I, taken as
subject, "is pure relation-to-itself in which we abstract from all conception
and feeling, from every state of mind, and every peculiarity of nature,
talent, and experience" (1968b:par. 20). In other words, Hegel defines pure
thought and pure being in exactly the same way. Both are simple self-
relation or mere relation-to-self. Pure thought and pure being are one. We
can approach this identity from two directions. From the side of being:
"Being [Sein] is not to be felt, or perceived by sense, or pictured in

imagination; it is pure thought" (1968b:par. 86). Or from the side of thought:

> In the 'I,' being is simply in myself; I can abstract from everything, but I cannot abstract from thought, for the abstracting is itself thought, it is the activity of the universal, simple relation-to-self. Being is exemplified in the very act of abstraction. I can indeed destroy myself, but that is the liberty to abstract from my existence. 'I am,'—in the 'I,' the 'am' is already included. (1968a:I, 124)

Hegel believes that this argument for the identity of pure thought and pure being expresses the rational meaning of the ontological argument anticipated by authors as different as Anselm, Descartes, and Spinoza. But his appreciation of the integral relationship among the three proofs of God's existence allows Hegel to discern a further dimension of the ontological argument overlooked by his predecessors. This final moment of his proof of God's existence brings the argument full circle.

Hegel has laid the groundwork for the culminating moment of the proof in his analysis of the first two arguments for God's existence. For teleological vision, the cosmos is an organic process under wise and powerful divine providence. This point can be made in terms more in keeping with the ontological proof by saying that the universe is the realization or the incarnation of divine *Logos*. "In other words, the world and finite things have issued from the fullness of divine thoughts and divine decrees" (1968b:par. 163). Thought or reason is not simply subjective, but is the active essence of objectivity. Reason (*Logos*) is *practical*, and hence the world is rational (*logical*)./16/

We can better understand this stage of Hegel's argument by examining more completely his view of end (*Zweck*)./17/ He explains:

> But in general end is to be taken as the *rational in its concrete existence*. It manifests *rationality* because it is the concrete notion, that holds the *objective difference within its absolute unity*. . . . It is the self-equal *universal* and this, as containing self-repellent negativity, is in the first instance universal, and therefore as yet *indeterminate, activity*; but because this is the negative relation to itself, it *determines* itself immediately, and gives itself the moment of *particularity*, which, as likewise the *totality of the form reflected into itself*, is *content* as against the *posited* differences of the form. Equally immediately this negativity, through its relation to itself, is absolute reflection of the form into itself and thus *individuality*. (1969:741)

In this difficult text, Hegel identifies "end" as "the rational in its concrete existence" or the "concrete notion." Elsewhere he points out that "the realized end is the posited unity of subjectivity and objectivity" (1968b:par. 210). This identity of notion and realized end, or of subjectivity and objectivity, is not simple or immediate, but is mediated by the notion's dynamic process of self-actualization. The end is "the notion-in-action, or

the active universal—the determinate and self-determining universal"
(1968b:par. 57)./18/ The process through which the active notion realizes
itself is tripartite. In itself (*an sich*) the notion is abstract or
indeterminate./19/ It remains a simple potentiality, or as Hegel puts it, "the
self-equal universal." This indeterminate notion, the abstract universal, is,
however, inherently self-contradictory. It is "self-repellent negativity," or
"negative relation-to-self." In less technical language, the notion realizes its
potential by determining itself concretely./20/ The actualization of the
notion presupposes its *objective* expression. In becoming itself, the active
notion repels itself from itself in the realm of objectivity. Object and subject
are not antithetical, for the object is the objective (*Zweck* as well as *objektiv*)
of the subject. The self-negation of the subjective notion is really its self-
realization as the objective notion. The determinate objectification of the
notion (its *Fürsichsein*) is the second moment of its self-actualization. In the
final phase of this process, the reunion of subjectivity and objectivity implicit
in the first two stages of the notion's becoming is realized explicitly./21/
Since objectivity is a necessary moment in the actuality of subjectivity, the
subject's relation to the object is its self-relation in which the otherness
(simple opposition) of subject and object is sublated. While objectivity is the
first negation of subjectivity, the subject's appropriation of the object as a
determinate expression (*Äusserung*) of itself is the negation of this negation
by means of which the subject returns to itself through the relation to its
"other." The actualization of the notion is a process of double negation in
which subjectivity and objectivity are completely reconciled./22/ Hegel
summarizes his point:

> The notion is this totality: the process, the movement of objectifying
> itself. . . . The notion, however, is all that is deepest and highest. The very
> idea of the notion implies that it has to sublate this defect of subjectivity,
> overcome this distinction between itself and being, and has to objectify itself.
> It is itself this act of producing itself as something which has being, as some-
> thing objective. Whenever we think of the notion, we must give up the idea
> that it is something which *we* only possess, and construct within ourselves.
> The notion is the soul, the end or goal of what is living. What we call soul is
> the notion, and in spirit, in consciousness, the notion as such attains to exis-
> tence as a free notion existing in its subjectivity as distinct from its reality as
> such. (1968a:III, 356–57)

While determinate being finds its truth in the notion, the notion
becomes actual in determinate being. Apart from its appearance in objectivity, subjectivity remains unreal. Thought and being realize themselves only
in and through each other. They form an inseparable dialectical unity apart
from which neither is, and through which each becomes itself. This unity of
subjectivity and objectivity, of notion and existence, of thought and being is
truth or the Absolute Idea.

> But having reached the result that the Idea is the unity of the notion and objectivity or in other words is the true, it must not be regarded merely as a *goal* to which we have to approximate but which itself always remains a kind of *beyond*; on the contrary, we must recognize that everything actual *is* only in so far as it possesses the Idea and expresses it. (1969:756)

The ontological proof reveals the world as the embodiment of the divine Idea, the incarnation of the *Logos* of God. God is the "essence [*Inbegriff*] of all reality" (1968b:par. 86). Through the comprehension of God as the Creator and Sustainer of the world and of the world as the self-realization of God, Creator and creation, God and man, infinite and finite, absolute necessity and contingency, subjectivity and objectivity are reconciled. The ontological argument grasps *(begreift)* rationally the truth represented *(vorgestellt)* by God's incarnation in Christ.

VI. Truth, Freedom, and Salvation

As the final moment of Hegel's proof of God's existence, the ontological argument takes up into itself and gives fuller expression to the truth of the cosmological and teleological arguments. However, here as elsewhere, the *Alpha* and the *Omega* are one. The cosmological and teleological arguments not only point toward, but also presuppose, the ontological argument. The two rhythms of the proof present different moments of the God-world relation. In the ontological argument, Hegel attempts to unfold the movement of God to world—to demonstrate that the divine *Logos* reveals itself through its appearance or incarnation in the world. He believes that this process at once discloses the identity and maintains the distinction of God and the world, of Father and Son. Jesus is fully God and fully man. Moreover, Hegel contends that the ontological argument manifests God's benevolence. The *Logos* becomes incarnate so that God and the world might be reconciled. The cosmological and teleological moments of the proof explore the movement of the world to God. These proofs would not be possible apart from the incarnation of the divine Logos. Had God left no footprints in the world,/23/ creation could not find its way back to Him. Through the cosmological and teleological arguments, one recognizes that the world is neither self-subsistent nor irrational, but is under the providential care of a creative power which is full of wisdom.

The *Itinerarium Mentis in Deum* and the *Descensus Dei im Mundi* are inseparable, for in the final analysis they are two moments of one complex movement. On the one hand, Hegel's threefold proof presents God's going and coming, His exodus from and return to Himself. Man's ascent and God's descent are two moments of a single process. From this perspective, man's knowledge of God is God's knowledge of Himself. In other words, through man's knowledge, God comes to self-consciousness. This divine self-consciousness is the highest stage of God's self-realization and is the *telos* of the entire cosmic process. On the other hand, absolute knowledge represents human fulfillment in which man overcomes estrangement by appropriating his atonement with God. Through comprehending the unity of the divine and the human, dialectical reason sees man's reconciliation with his "Other" as his reconciliation with himself. Self-realization that is mediated by the relationship to otherness is the nullification of heteronomy and the assertion of autonomy./24/ To be fully self-determined within the structure of relation to "otherness" is to be genuinely free. Hegel completes his interpretation of the proof of God's existence by equating the freedom dialectical reason brings with human salvation./25/

> For thinking means that in the other, one meets with oneself. It means a liberation, which is not the flight of abstraction, but consists in that which is actual having itself not as something else, but as its own being and creation, in the other actuality with which it is bound up by the force of necessity. As existing for oneself, this liberation is called I; as developed to its totality, it is free spirit; as feeling, it is love; and as enjoyment, it is salvation. (1968b:par. 8)

The Hegelian system is a sustained effort to lead the reader from incomplete understanding to absolute knowledge. Hegel intends the course he charts to be the conceptual articulation of the truth represented, but not rationally comprehended by the three traditional proofs of God's existence. Through the identification of absolute knowledge with salvation, Hegel suggests that his intricate philosophical system is nothing less than the *Intinerarium Mentis in Deum*. The end awaiting those who undertake this arduous journey is the negation of alienation and the realization of reconciliation.

> The reconciliation is achieved, when the will in its result returns to the presupposition of knowledge. In other words, it consists in the unity of the theoretical and the practical Idea. Will knows the end to be its own, and intelligence apprehends the world as the actualized notion. This is the true attitude of rational knowledge. Nothingness and transitoriness constitute only the superficial features and not the true essence of the world. That essence is the notion in and for itself; and thus the world is the Idea. All unsatisfied endeavor ceases, when we recognize that the final purpose of the world is accomplished no less than ever accomplishing itself. Generally speaking, this is the man's way of looking; while the young imagine that the world is utterly sunk in wickedness, and that the first thing needful is a thorough transformation. The religious mind views the world as ruled by Divine Providence, and therefore as corresponding to what it ought to be. (1968b:par. 234)

For Hegel, the enjoyment of this reconciliation is the peace that passes all (analytic) understanding.

Notes

/1/   Although Kant distinguishes reason and understanding, Hegel does not believe Kant transcends the categories of analytic understanding. Nevertheless he acknowledges two points at which Kant's thought moves in the direction of dialectical reason. The first is his consideration of the Antinomies in the First Critique, and the second is his discussion of inner teleology in the Third Critique.

/2/   At the completion of the *Itinerarium Mentis in Deum*, one recognizes that the converse likewise obtains: the ontological argument is incomplete and incorrect without the cosmological and teleological proofs. God achieves fulfillment only in and through the exercise of his creative power and his incarnation in creation. The precise way in which the ontological proof presupposes the cosmological and teleological moments will be considered in our discussion of the relation of thought and being. (See section 5.)

/3/   Throughout his discussion of this proof, Hegel uses "contingent" and "finite" and "necessary" and "infinite" interchangeably. We shall follow Hegel's usage. The rationale for this identification should become apparent as the analysis unfolds.

/4/   It is helpful to keep in mind that *"zufällig"* carries the connotation "accidental," while *"notwendig"* implies essential.

/5/   The careful reader will have noticed that a dialectical analysis of finitude discloses the same structure of self-reference through relation to other that we now see in infinitude. To the extent that a determinate entity realizes itself through its other, it sublates its finitude and particularity in infinity. Self-referential double negation is the structure of infinitude that realizes itself through finitude. Finitude *is* only to the extent that it participates in or is an appearance of the infinite process of double negation. This interpretation of the interrelation of infinity and finitude is consistent with the insightful analysis of this problem developed by Anselm Min (1976). Min's discussion helps to clarify the argument we have been elaborating. "It is the very nature of the finite as such to determine itself to be finite, contingent, and thus inclusive of an Other from within in the very definition of its own being. This is to say that the finite not only negates, relates, and transcends itself to an Other and is thus mediated by an Other, but also negates the first negation, relates to itself the first transcendence toward an Other, thus mediating itself to itself by canceling the otherness of the Other which limits it. Only thus is the finite truly finite, truly itself. This means, however, that the finite is not merely itself but contains an Other of itself in its very being. The finite is both itself and its Other, the infinite, and can be finite only as this unity of itself and its Other, of nonbeing and being" (73).

/6/   Hegel credits Kant (especially in the Third Critique) with having identified the concept of inner teleology. But he criticizes Kant for insisting that this notion is simply a subjective regulative idea that is not necessarily constitutive of objective reality.

/7/   Thus Hegel does not interpret the whole simply as the sum total of all parts. Therefore he avoids the hermeneutical impasse of not being able to know anything until he knows everything.

/8/   The rationale for Hegel's use of "subject" or "subjectivity" in this context will become evident in our analysis of the ontological argument.

/9/   If we recall the similarity between the proofs and Hegel's logic, we can see that this movement from the cosmological, through the teleological, to the ontological proof parallels the progression from being, through essence, to notion. Objectivity in itself passes over into subjectivity.

/10/   Hegel does not present a form of the ontological argument that conforms to analytic understanding, as he does for the cosmological and teleological arguments. In this case, he is content to explain that undialectical reflection simply cannot comprehend the ontological proof.

/11/   At this point analytic understanding's most devastating shortcoming becomes apparent. It can never attain knowledge or discover truth. Objectivity remains an ungraspable beyond (an unknowable thing-in-itself) for subjectivity. Hegel believes the Kantian critical philosophy to be a paradigm of such a position. Kant's failure to establish knowledge (the certain identity of subject and object) is of a piece with his inability to comprehend the speculative significance of the proofs of God's existence.

/12/   Recalling our discussion of the relation between finitude and infinity, we now see that the structure of subjectivity is isomorphic with the true structure of objectivity. The subject, as well as the object, is the internal contradiction of identity-within-difference, a pluralized unity, and a unified plurality. Subjectivity and objectivity express the relation-to-other or the dialectical relation-to-other or the dialectical structure of double negativity. Therefore when Hegel argues that the subject finds *itself* in the object, he means that in the true comprehension of objectivity, subjectivity sees itself reflected.

/13/   This internal structure of consciousness is not immediately apparent. The thinking subject initially hypostatizes its concrete determinations as objects independent of itself. Consequently not only is there implicit opposition within the thinking self, there is also an explicit split between thought and object (being). As should be apparent by now, the ontological argument and speculative philosophy as a whole seek to overcome this breach.

/14/   Elsewhere Hegel explains: "In fact, I am this pure thought, and the 'I' itself is indeed the very expression of it, for 'I' as such is this abstract identity of myself within myself as wholly without determination—'I' as 'I' am merely thought as that which is posited with the determination of subjective existence reflected into itself—I am *the thinking* [*das Denkende*]" (1968a:II, 32).

/15/   This implies, of course, that the thinking I is concrete universality. Our consideration of the teleological argument has already shown the truth of determinate being to be its relation to the whole of which it is a member, or its concrete universality. This structural homology between subjectivity and objectivity emerges explicitly in the next part of Hegel's interpretation of the ontological argument. For the moment, he is concerned to establish the identity of *pure* thought and *abstract* being.

/16/   Hegel seeks here to express the speculative import of Kant's insight into the practical nature of reason. In attempting to understand Hegel's analysis, it is important to recognize that he agrees with Kant's basic identification of practical reason and free will.

/17/ "*Zweck*," of course, also connotes "goal," "aim," "purpose," and "design."

/18/ As will become apparent, the universality of the notion is the common relation by which its particular determinations are bound together and in which they acquire their specific identity.

/19/ It is precisely this aspect of the notion that earlier forms of the ontological argument take as their central focus, and upon which the first part of Hegel's discussion of this proof concentrates.

/20/ We must keep in mind that in this context reason is practical or active. Hegel's complex analysis might become clearer if we consider the common example of purposive human activity. Intentional action consists of three moments. In the first place, one imagines an end or goal to be realized. At this stage, the end is potential—it lacks concrete actuality. In order to overcome this indeterminacy, one must struggle to effect (*wirken*) his purpose, or to express his intention objectiviely. This is the second phase of purposive action. The final moment of this process is the appropriation of actuality (*Wirklichkeit*) as the effect (*Wirkung*) of one's intentional activity. The realized goal is the objective existence of one's subjective idea (or ideal). In completed purposive activity, ideality is real and reality is ideal. Rational reflection comprehends objectivity as the external reflection of subjectivity. In brief, intentional action unites subjectivity and objectivity.

/21/ This is the notion's *Anundfürsichsein*, or as we shall see, the Absolute Idea.

/22/ The structural relation between subjectivity and objectivity that we have been exploring is the bare dialectical skeleton of both Feuerbach's critique of religious belief and of Marx's influential analysis of self-alienation and reconciliation in the labor process.

/23/ This image is taken from Bonaventure's *Itinerarium Mentis in Deum*, the work from which the title of this essay is borrowed. Our analysis of Hegel's position should have revealed his deep affinities with this mystical strand of Western theology.

/24/ In contrast to analytic understanding's interpretation of autonomy as independence and separation from otherness, this form of autonomy presupposes internal relation to otherness. For dialectical reason, analytic understanding's view of autonomy remains alienated from, and therefore determined by, otherness—it is, in fact, heteronomy or bondage. Freedom arises through the comprehension of relation to other as self-relation necessary for self-realization. According to Hegel, this is authentic, rather than specious, autonomy.

/25/ At this point, Hegel integrates the theoretical, practical, and religious dimensions of experience in a manner that sets him apart both from Kant's placement of religion solely within the domain of practical reason, and from theologians and philosophers such as Schleiermacher, Jacobi, Coleridge, and Kierkegaard, for whom religion is a sphere distinct from the theoretical and practical realms.

Works Consulted

Kant, Immanuel
1973   *The Critique of Judgment.* Trans. J. C. Meredith. New York: Oxford University Press.

Min, Anselm
1976   "Hegel's Absolute: Transcendent or Immanent?" *Journal of Religion*, Volume 56, Number 1, pp. 68–87.

Hegel, G. W. F.
1968a   *Lectures on the Philosophy of Religion.* Trans. E. B. Spiers and J. B. Sanderson. New York: Humanities Press.
1968b   *The Logic of Hegel.* Trans. W. Wallace. New York: Oxford University Press.
1969   *Science of Logic.* Trans. A. V. Miller. New York: Humanities Press.
1970   *Werke in zwanzig Bänden.* Frankfurt: Suhrkamp Verlag.

Tillich, Paul
1964   *Theology of Culture.* New York: Oxford University Press.

Toward an Ontology of Relativism

I. Word and Silence

Expressing both an acute awareness of the contemporary theologian's quandary and the conviction that theological reflection remains possible in a post-modern world, Thomas Altizer recently has written: "Little that is overtly theological is actually hearable or speakable today. However, this situation can make possible the realization of a new theological language, a theological language which will speak by way of the voice or the voices of our time" (3–4). There can be little doubt that theology is in disarray. Since the decline in the fortunes of Neo-orthodoxy, certainty about the nature and viability of the theological enterprise has waned. Absence of the Word has left theological voices either silent or confused. If theological language is again to be speakable and hearable, the sources of silence must be penetrated and the depths of confusion plumbed. In the following pages, we shall explore the possibility that the paralysis of the theological imagination has been contracted by an increasing awareness of perspectival relativism.

II. Words and Silence

The roots of the contemporary recognition of relativism lie deep within eighteenth and nineteenth century theological and philosophical movements and are inseparably entangled with the psycho-social pluralization endemic to the process of modernization. Having gradually become persuaded that consciousness and therefore knowledge bear the indelible impress of the multiple situating forces that converge upon the cognitive activity of the knowing subject, many twentieth century theologians have been forced to address dilemmas posed by what they understand to be epistemological relativism./1/ Although the responses to the historicization of consciousness have been multiple, it is possible to identify three fundamental tendencies that have been particularly important for theological reflection.

Not infrequently, the apprehension of the situational character of knowledge and truth stills the voice of constructive systematic theology and directs attention to the study of religion as an historical human phenomenon. Uncertain of the tenability of normative assertions, the student attempts to bracket questions of truth and value through the assumption of the apparently non-judgmental stance of disinterested or objective investigation. The "scientific" study of religion often draws upon methodological principles defined by what Ricoeur lately has labeled the "hermeneutics of suspicion." From this perspective, consciousness in general, and religious consciousness in particular, is regarded as fundamentally epiphenomenal— rooted in or a reflection of more primordial natural, psychological, historical, and/or socio-economic processes. Inquiry attempts to identify the nature of latent sources of religious thought and practice. In other words, the activity of interpretation involves the effort to demystify the manifest content of consciousness through its reduction to the morphological base from which it originates and upon which it continues to rest. Apart from such demystification, consciousness, it is argued, remains false. While it is impossible to deny the significance of insights generated by the psychology, sociology, anthropology, history, and philosophy of religion, it is necessary to recognize the limitations of this mode of analysis. In the first place, the very philosophical movements from which this general approach to the phenomenon of religion derives suggest the problematic character of ostensibly objective, value-free inquiry. Upon closer consideration, it becomes evident that objectivity is not disinterested, but reflects consent to specifiable values that carry with them important philosophical presuppositions and metaphysical implications (see Gouldner:35–52). Secondly, although insistent upon the need to demystify religious awareness, hermeneuticists of suspicion often have a tendency to reify latent layers of consciousness in a fashion analogous to the absolutization of consciousness' manifest content in the primary naiveté of believers. When this course is followed, the hermeneutics of suspicion is, paradoxically, insufficiently sensitive to perspectival relativism. Rather than uncovering the multi-dimensionality of religious expression, this type of scientific study of religion tends to become simplistically reductionistic. Probing potential shortcomings of hermeneutical suspicion, Ricoeur maintains: "Over against illusion and the fable-making function, demystifying hermeneutics sets up the rude discipline of necessity. It is the lesson of Spinoza: one first finds himself free within understood necessity. . . . But, in return, does not this discipline of the real, this ascesis of the necessary lack the grace of imagination, the upsurge of the possible? And does not this grace of imagination have something to do with the Word as Revelation?" (1970:35–36).

"The Word as Revelation" forms the basis of an alternative (and opposite) response to perspectival relativism. Recognizing the seemingly inevitable progression from the inward turn of Schleiermacher's theological method to the psycho-social reductionism of Feuerbach and Marx, Karl Barth insisted that theological reflection perpetually focus on the absolute and transcendent Word of God, rather than on subjective structures of religious awareness. Barth agreed with the relativistic interpretation of human religion, but rejected the applicability of such analysis to the Word of God revealed in Christ. The divine Word is the creative self-disclosure of God, and not the sinful self-projection of man. For Barth, the only way to overcome the anomie of relativism was by obedience to or belief in Christian revelation. Hence what Barth affirmed of all religious traditions, he denied of Christian faith *sensu eminentiori*.

It should be apparent, however, that Barth's answer to relativism is inadequate. His program consisted of a sustained effort to reassert the inviolability of Christianity and to insulate Christian belief from the type of scrutiny and interpretation to which all other forms of human thought and action are justifiably subjected. Barth responded to the confusion born of pluralism by the reaffirmation of a radical monotheism that seeks to provide a single center of value which effectively structures experience and integrates personality. But what if Yeats is right?

> Turning and turning in the widening gyre
> The falcon cannot hear the falconer:
> Things fall apart; the centre cannot hold;
> Mere anarchy is loosed upon the world.

It appears that Barth counseled a return to pre-critical naiveté which no longer seems possible for many moderns. Our course must pass through instead of around relativism.

A final noteworthy development on the contemporary theological scene illustrates Peter Berger's contention that "every modern society must find some way to come to terms with the process of pluralization. Very probably this will entail some form of legitimation of at least a certain measure of plurality" (69). In direct opposition to Neo-orthodoxy's exclusively monotheistic response to relativism, there recently has been a reemergence of polytheistic religiosity. Instead of seeing in religious, social, and psychological pluralism a problem to be overcome, polytheists regard it as an occasion for the enrichment of the human spirit. David Miller explains: "When released from the tyrannical imperialism of monotheism by the death of God, man has the opportunity of discovering new dimensions hidden in the depths of reality's history. He may discover a new freedom to acknowledge variousness and many-sidedness" (3; see also Ogilvy, 1977). Although Miller recognizes the disorientation wrought by the loss of a stable center, he insists that "after the fright passes, one notices a new sense of liberty: . . . everywhere one stands is a center, a new center, and the universe of meaning is not limited to a tight little horizon, a vicious circle of a single mind and lifetime" (11). Polytheism endeavors to offer religious legitimation for psychosocial pluralism and perspectival relativism. "The multiple patterns of polytheism allow room to move meaningfully through a pluralistic universe. They free one to affirm the radical plurality of the self. . . . But polytheism is not only a social reality, it is also a philosophical condition. It is that reality experienced by men and women when Truth with a capital 'T' cannot be articulated reflectively according to a single grammar, a single logic, or a single symbol-system" (ix, 4).

This new polytheism, however, is as unsatisfactory as old forms of monotheism. It swings from the extreme of distinct self-integration and social, cultural, and religious intolerance to the opposite extreme of personal multiplicity and social, cultural, and religious dis-integration. We are asked to choose between the suffocation of blind faith and rigid ego, and the confusion of a plurality of beliefs and a protean personality, which carried to its logical conclusion is the negation of human consciousness./2/ In addition to this, polytheism's uncritical inclusiveness renders problematic theoretical discrimination and practical judgment. Though intending the opposite, polytheism borders on nihilism. Finally, on a metaphysical level, both polytheism and monotheism are equally undialectical. The former emphasizes plurality to the exclusion of unity, and the latter stresses unity at the expense of plurality. What neither polytheists nor monotheists grasp is the dialectical relationship between unity and plurality in which identity and difference come to be through each other.

In sum, the major attempts to resolve the dilemmas posed by perspectival relativism appear to be inadequate. All too often words of contemporary theologians bespeak silence rather than Word. This failure is, in large measure, the result of the uncritical acceptance or rejection of epistemological relativism. A revitalization of the theological impulse requires a more careful exploration of the metaphysical implications of relativism than has yet been undertaken./3/ The remainder of this essay is devoted to an attempt to demonstrate that relativism is mandated *both* epistemologically and ontologically. What has gone unnoticed is that the discovery of truth's relativity is the realization of its inherently dialectical character. Truth is relative because meaning is contextual and being is relational. Contextualized meaning and relational being join in relative truth disclosed through symbolic awareness. It must be stressed, however, that the claim of truth to be relative does not necessarily involve either its denial or the simple assertion of multiple and conflicting truths. Meaning, as being itself, assumes determinate form through reciprocal relationship in which co-implicates mutually constitute each other. This line of argument turns upon a distinction between the interpretation of relativity in terms of dialectical relationality and the more common notion of relativity as the subjectivization of all knowledge./4/ Careful reflection suggests that the claim of the thoroughgoing subjectivity of truth is negated in the very effort to affirm it./5/ The recognition of the bond joining relativistic epistemology and relational ontology points to a way out of this paradox of subjectivity by enabling us to see truth aborning through the intercourse of truths. As the argument unfolds, it will become apparent that the only thing that is not relative is relativity itself. What remains constant amid the relativity of perspectives is constitutive relationality—a claim that is affirmed in the very effort to negate it. This point can be made in a more provocative, and doubtless more problematic, way. Dialectical vision discerns the necessary interplay of relativity and its contrary, absoluteness. Relativity can establish itself only in and through its opposite—that which is not relative, the absolute. Conversely, absoluteness can constitute itself only in and through its opposite—that which is not absolute, the relative. So understood relativity and absoluteness are not simply antithetical, but mutually coinhere. Absoluteness is the structure of relation by means of which determinate identities establish and maintain themselves. Neither relata nor relationship can exist without the other. In a more theological idiom, God and world cannot exist apart from one another. God forever becomes incarnate, and the finite is always in the process of becoming reconciled with the infinite. The absolutizing of relativity is at the same time the relativizing of absoluteness. These are but two dimensions of a unified epistemological-ontological process./6/

III. Contextualization of Meaning

Meaning is contextual; context is semiophantic. "Meaning," writes Norman O. Brown, "is in the play, or the interplay of light . . . in the irridescence, the interplay, in the interconnections: at the intersections, at the crossroads" (246–47). Seeing is always seeing with—effecting a contrast. Any angle of vision is mediated by, or arises through its relation to alternative viewpoints. Taken alone, particular meaning is not simply false, but is completely indefinable, or thoroughly unspecifiable. The contextualization of meaning is dis-covered through dialectical reflection. When grasped dialectically, it is clear that perspectives depend upon each other for self-definition, and therefore are internally related and mutually constitutive rather than disjunctively opposed to one another. With this insight, we glimpse the end toward which our argument is directed: context is the creatrix of meaning— meaning is constituted by the specific context within which it is con-figured. It is necessary, however, to consider more completely the nature of contextual relations ingredient in meaning. A diagrammatic representation should simplify our task.

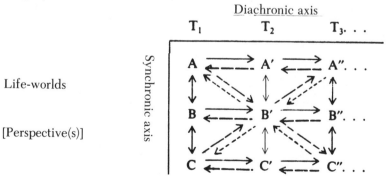

Diachronic axis

T_1 T_2 T_3. . .

Life-worlds

[Perspective(s)]

Synchronic axis

A ⇄ A′ ⇄ A″. . .

B ⇄ B′ ⇄ B″. . .

C ⇄ C′ ⇄ C″. . .

In attempting to ascertain the dialectical dimensions of meaning, a distinction must be drawn, for analytical purposes, between diachronic and synchronic relationality. The diachronic axis of the diagram charts moments of temporal process (T_1, T_2, T_3. . . ; A, A', A''. . . ; B, B', B''. . . ; and C, C', C''. . .). Though distinguishable, these moments are caught in a complex web of recollection/repetition, concrescence/realization, and anticipation/ intension. The synchronic axis of the diagram depicts phenomena/7/ co-extant at any particular moment of temporal process (A, B, C; A', B', C'; and A''; B''; C''). While diachronism refers to temporal unfolding, synchronism points to simultaneity of occurrence. Vectors joining identifiable moments and specifiable actualities and/or potentialities indicate on the one hand, the interplay of temporal ecstases and the inseparability of synchronous phenomena, and on the other hand, the thoroughly dialectical relationship between diachronism and synchronism. As the separation of any instant from other temporal moments or the isolation of a certain particularity from coexisting particularities represents artificial abstraction, so the effort to consider diachronic and synchronic relations apart from one another inevitably leads to fundamental epistemological and ontological distortions and to problematic theological and philosophical conclusions. With respect to semantics, the context determinative of meaning consists of contrasts among alternative perspectives extant at a particular time and of relations among dialectical moments of historically developing *Lebensanschauungen*. If our argument is to become persuasive, synchronicity and diachronicity must be examined in more detail.

Conceptual meaning comes to expression through "the interplay of sameness and difference" (Ricoeur, 1973:109). Reference to otherness is not extrinsic and accidental, but is intrinsic and essential to the determination of specific meaning. In fine, meaning is thoroughly dialectical or completely relational. It is important to note, however, that sameness and difference are contradictories that reciprocally interpenetrate one another. Our diagram helps us to see this point more clearly. Within the synchronic axis, the meaning of B' at temporal moment T_2 is constituted by its relation to A' and C'. Apart from association with otherness, B' remains completely indeterminate and utterly meaning-less. B''s meaning is defined by its conjunction with and distinction from A' and C'. In more general terms to be elaborated in the following ontological analysis, identity is difference from difference, the negation of negation that is simultaneously self-affirmation. When we recognize that B' can represent a particular life-world or symbolic system, it becomes apparent that the synchronic contextualization of meaning entails perspectival relativism. Since A', B', and C' are co-implicates, the meaning of each is relative to the other./8/

If artificially reified, however, synchronicity implies a factitious arrest of the historical development depicted by the diachronic axis of our diagram. Meaning is also subject to temporal dialectics; it emerges or unfolds through time. Since temporal ecstases overlay one another, synchronic and diachronic relations are inseparable. Past, present, and future are not isolable, but thoroughly interpenetrate and mutually condition each other. "My present," Merleau-Ponty argues, "outruns itself in the direction of an immediate future and immediate past and impinges upon them where they actually are, namely in the past and in the future themselves" (418). Or, as Stephen Crites insists, "an experienced present is not simply a dissociated 'now' but contains at least a vestige of memory and a leaning into anticipation" (32). The recognition of the creative intercourse among the three temporal ecstases must not, however, obscure the distinction between the relation of the present to the past and to the future. The past is generated by the accumulation of activated potency and forms an ever-receding horizon of present experience. The weight of the past bears on the present and presses toward the future. In turning toward the past, the present attempts to dis-cover its own facticity. The past is not completely circumscribed, but extends into the present and the future, thereby exerting determinative influence. But time is a two way street—present and future are not simply the unfolding of the past. Merleau-Ponty correctly maintains that "the future is not prepared behind the observer, it is a brooding presence moving to meet him like a storm" (411). The future invades the present and penetrates the past. Through anticipatory reach, the present encounters the storm gathering on the ever-invading horizon of the future. The intension of the future eventuates the present and reconstructs the past. The passage of the time grows out of the past passing through the present into the future, and the future passing through the present into the past. While extending past guards temporal continuity, impending future grounds freedom and insures novelty./9/ The present is the "crossroads," the "intersection" of past and future in which the horizons of sedimenting past and imploding future overlap. H. Ganse Little summarizes our point concisely.

> The present drives 'like a wedge' into both the receding past and the outstanding future only because it is concommitantly invaded by accumulating past and arching toward the future and an impending future arching toward the past. Conversely, the future impends and the past accumulates only because the present is anticipative and recollective. There is no route to a position beyond the puzzle of this primordial reciprocity. Historicality, although multiform and dialectically 'ecstatic,' swings on a single hinge—the coinherence of past, present and future. (16–17)

Due to the dialectical structure of temporality, meaning is necessarily historical and perpetually revisable. It is unfinished, yet always refinishing. Since the present is the "middest" (Kermode) distended between beginning and end, meaning is born of the tension generated by the interplay of retention and protension./10/ Returning to our example, the meaning of B' is integrally related to its own past (B) and future (B″). Discernment of the meaning of B′ requires archaeological and teleological reflection that grasps its internal relation to B and B″. Since time is an ongoing process of negation/11/ or unchanging change, meaning is never static, but is perpetually emergent. The meaning of the past belongs to the future, and the future incarnates constitutive reverberations resounding through the past. Because meaning evolves with the passage of time, it remains transitional, is constantly re-forming. The articulation of meaning presupposes unending temporal re-visioning. The diachronic contextualization of meaning points toward the temporal or historical relativity of truth.

In order to complete our consideration of the contextual character of meaning, it is necessary to join more closely our synchronic and diachronic analyses. We have discovered that the meaning of B′ is constituted on the one hand by relation to A′ and C′, and on the other hand by relation to B and B″. Through the extension of our synchronic investigation of co-existent perspectives at T_2 to moments T_1 and T_3, it becomes clear that the meaning of B and B″ grows out of their relations to A/C and A″/C″ respectively. Moreover, it should be evident that our diachronic analysis of the dialectical interplay of B, B′, and B″ also applies to A, A′, and A″ and to C, C′, and C″. These insights lead to the inference that the confluence of synchronic and diachronic relationality establishes a mediate (rather than a direct) relation between B′ and A, C, A″, and C″. For example, B′ is drawn into indirect relation with A through direct relation to A′ and B (indicated by dotted vectors AB′/B′A), etc./12/ These indirect relations form the final factor contributing to the meaning of B′. Our overall analysis leads to the conclusion that the meaning of B′ is a function of the concrescence of the dynamically developing contextual field of which it is an integral member./13/

The contextualization of meaning unearths the roots of perspectival relativism. Meaning assumes form through dialectical interrelationship in which co-implicates mutually constitute each other. Synchronic relations among simultaneously appearing perspectives and diachronic relations among temporally unfolding *Lebensanschauungen* reveal the inexhaustability and ceaseless revisability of meaning./14/ As the reader may suspect, however, a further problem lurks beneath the surface of our analysis. Though the contextualization of meaning might make sense, has it any reference?

IV. Relationality of Being

Our exploration of perspectival relativism has led to the recognition of the synchronic and diachronic relations intrinsic to determinant meaning. However, if our argument is to have more than semantic significance, we must turn our attention from matters of epistemology and hermeneutics to ontological analysis. Having probed the contextualization of meaning, we must attempt to establish the socialization of being.

According to Wallace Stevens, "Nothing is itself taken alone. Things are because of interrelations or interactions" (163). Stevens' rich insight points the direction for further reflection. Whereas our previous task involved overcoming logical atomism through dialectical reason, we now seek to sublate ontological substantialism and monadicism in relational ontology. Neither a radical monism nor an extreme pluralism represents an adequate metaphysical position. Monism tends to hypostatize purely abstract, self-identical substance (often defined as *Sein*, Being-itself, or Being-in-general) as the ontologically prior foundation of all reality in such a way that difference or plurality is reduced to accidental, insubstantial status. Monadicism, on the contrary, absolutizes difference or multiplicity and consequently renders unity and integration epiphenomenal. Though representing contrasting metaphysical viewpoints, monism and pluralism rest on the common assumption of the irreconcilable opposition between unity and plurality, identity and difference. Having established an artificial either-or, one is forced to choose between two apparently incompatible alternatives. While monism (like monotheism) accents unity over multiplicity, pluralism (like polytheism) stresses multiplicity to the exclusion of unity. Neither perspective recognizes the interconnection of oneness and manyness through which each is constituted by relation to the other. An identity-within-difference and a difference-within-identity; pluralized unity and unified plurality—such is the ontological base of perspectival relativism reflected in contextualized meaning./15/

A more careful consideration of identity and difference promises disclosure of the relationality of being. Not uncommonly, particular existents are regarded as essentially discrete and primordially separate from one another. Accordingly, identity is believed to be established through self-relation independent of reference-to-other. Relations to different subsistences are external to the antecedently constituted entity and therefore remain accidental to determinate being. From this viewpoint, identity and difference are indifferent. But this line of interpretation is seriously misleading, for identity and difference are inseparably bound in a dialectical relation of co-implication. Altizer is correct when he points out that "we can evoke an actual or real identity only by embodying difference, a real and actual difference, a difference making identity manifest, and making it manifest as itself. Only the presence of difference calls identity forth, and it calls it forth in its difference from itself, in its difference from an identity which is eternally the same" (37). In other terms, being-for-self *necessarily* entails being-for-other. That which "is equal to itself and is for-itself is such only in its absolute difference from every other. And this difference implies a relation with other things, a relation that is the cessation of its being-for-itself" (Hyppolite:116). As Hegel argued in the second chapter of his *Phänomenologie des Geistes*, any concrete "thing is set up as having a being of its own, as existing for itself, or as an absolute negation of all otherness; hence it is absolute negation merely relating itself to itself. But this kind of negation is the sublation of itself, or means that it has its essential reality in another" (174). Since determinate entities are co-relative, otherness ceases to be merely other and difference no longer is indifferent. Relation-to-other is simultaneously mediate self-relation in which concrete identity is established and maintained. Simple difference is abrogated with the recognition that it is through "its opposition that the thing relates itself to others, and is *essentially* this relation and only this. The relation, however, is the negation of its independence. . . ." (Hegel, 1967:174)./16/ Relations are internal and essential, rather than external and accidental. Any "object [or person] is really in one and the same respect the opposite of itself—for itself 'so far as' it is for another, and for another 'so far as' it is for itself. It is for itself, reflected into self, one; but all this is asserted along with its opposite, with its being for another, and for that reason is asserted merely to be sublated. In other words, this existence for itself is as much unessential as that which alone was meant to be unessential, viz. the relation to another" (Hegel, 1967:175). As we move from analytical abstraction to dialectical reflection, we discern the relationality of being. In short, our analysis supports Stevens' contention that "Things are because of interrelations or interactions." Relation is ontologically constitutive—to be is to be related. An extended text from Hegel's *Wissenschaft der Logik* summarizes the insight toward which we have been moving.

> Thus something *through its own nature* relates itself to the other, because otherness is posited in it as its own moment; its being-within-self includes the negation within it, by means of which alone it now has its affirmative determinate being. But the other is also qualitatively distinguished from this and is thus posited outside the something. The negation of its other is now the quality of the something, for it is as this sublating of its other that it is something. It is only in this sublation that the other is really opposed to another determinate being; the other is only externally opposed to another determinate being; the other is only externally opposed to the *first* something, or rather, since in fact they are *directly* connected, . . . their connection is this, that determinate being has *passed over* into otherness, something into other, and something is just as much an other as the other itself is. Now insofar as the being-with-self is the non-being of the otherness which is contained in it but which at the same time has a distinct being of its own, the something is itself the negation, *the ceasing of an other in it*; it is posited as relating itself negatively to the other and in so doing preserving itself; this other, the being-within-self of the something as negation of the negation, is its *in-itself*, and at the same time this sublation is *present in it* as a simple negation, namely as its negation of the other something external to it. (1969:125–26)

We might fruitfully return to the diagram previously employed. Since our concern at this point is ontological rather than semantic, the letters represent particular phenomena such as concrete actualities and/or imaginable possibilities./17/ For the sake of consistency, let us once more focus on B' (though the same mode of analysis could be applied to any depicted phenomenon). The previous shape of the argument gathered in the foregoing pages persuades us that the determinate identity of B' can be said to be posited by its relation to other objects in the field of which it is a member. Again it is helpful to distinguish synchronic and diachronic dimensions of relationality. Considering the synchronic axis, we see that the actuality of B' grows out of its intrinsic relation to otherness, in this instance to A' and C'. Given the dialectical bond between identity and difference, it is evident that B' "through its own nature relates itself to the other"—to A' and C'. Relations are not added to discrete subsistences by the cognitive activity of a subject, but are ontologically ingredient in all determinate phenomena. Apart from internal relation to difference, B' is no-thing. In-itself B' presupposes reference-to-other. There is (nothing) no thing-in-itself, for self-relation is always mediated by relation-to-other./18/ Moreover, although synchronic and diachronic relations are, as we have seen, distinguishable, they are ontologically inseparable. Being, never static, is always in the process of unfolding—of becoming./19/ Consequently, determinate identity is forged both by association with phenomena coexistent at a given time, and by thoroughgoing situatedness within temporal-historical process. From the examination of the diachronic axis of our diagram, we recognize that B' is informed by relation to B and B'' and by indirect conjunction with A, C, A'', and C''. The emergent character of the diachronic constituting field implies that the actuality of B' develops gradually. Identity is never completely established, a *fait accompli*; it is always arriving, always coming-to-be, always be-coming. Identity is not immutable, but is dynamic, temporal, historical.

The synchronic and diachronic components of relationality are joined by isomorphic morphology. More specifically, negativity is the structure of both synchronic relations among co-existents and of diachronic relations among temporally developing phenomena. As our borrowings from Hegel suggest, negativity is the structural foundation of constitutive relationality. The affirmation of identity is mediated by the negation of otherness that itself is negative. In keeping with Spinoza, "*omnis determinatio est negatio.*" In other words, the formation of determinate being involves a process of double negation in which essential relation to otherness is created and sustained. "Thus something *through its own nature* relates itself to the other, because otherness is posited in it as its own moment; its being-within-self includes the negation within it, by means of which alone it now has its affirmative determinate being" (Hegel, 1969:125). Returning to our diagram, we realize that A', C', A, B, A'', B'' and C'' represent the negation of B', or are non-B'. Briefly stated, B' *is* the negation/non-being of non-B'. Affirmation is at the same time negation, and being is simultaneously non-being.

> The positive is positedness as reflected into self-likeness; but what is reflected
> is positedness, that is, the negation as negation, and so this reflection-into-self
> has reference-to-other for its determination. The negative is positedness as
> reflected into unlikeness; but the positedness is unlikeness with itself and
> absolute self-reference. Each is the whole; the positedness reflected into
> unlikeness-to-self also contains likeness. . . . Each is itself and its other;
> consequently each has *its determinateness* not in an other, but *in its own
> self*. Each is self-referred, and the reference to its other is only a self-
> reference. This has a twofold aspect; each is a reference to its non-being is
> only a moment in it. But on the other hand positedness here has become a
> being; an indifferent subsistence; consequently, the other of itself which each
> contains is also the non-being of that in which it is supposed to be contained
> only as a moment. Each therefore *is*, only insofar as its *non-being* is, and is in
> an identical relationship with it. . . . In the first place, then each *is*, *only
> insofar as the other is*; it is what it is, through the other, through its own non-
> being; it is only a *positedness*; secondly, it is *insofar as the other is not*; it is
> what it is, through the *reflection-into-self*. But these two are the *one*
> mediation of the opposition as such, in which they are simply only *posited
> moments*. (Hegel, 1969:424–25)

Expressed in less technical terms, presence is present as absence, or with
Altizer, "presence becomes absence, and becomes actual as absence, and the
absence is the self-enactment of presence" (88). Instead of "to be *or* not to
be," the sum of the matter is to be *and* not to be, for to be is not to be, and
not to be is to be.

Although helpful, the circumscription of our diagrammatic representation can be misleading. The relational ontology we have been unfolding is,
in the final analysis, holistic. Something assumes *complete* concretion and
full self-realization only through its internal relation to the whole of which it
is a part. This whole, it must be emphasized, is not abstract and does not
exist in isolation from its parts. "There is nothing in the whole which is not
in the parts, and nothing in the parts which is not in the whole. The whole is
not abstract unity, but unity as a diverse manifold; but this unity, as that in
which the elements of the manifold are related to one another, is the
determinateness of each element through which it is a part. The relation
has, therefore, an inseparable identity and one self-subsistence" (Hegel,
1969:515–16)./20/ The whole is the self-identical structure of relationality
that assumes concrete actuality through the particularities whose determinate identities it establishes and maintains./21/

Our ontological reflection leads to the conclusion that being is fundamentally social, essentially relational. Determinate identity is born of ontological intercourse with otherness. The whole ingredient in and constituted
by particular entities is a self-differentiating totality that evolves
historically./22/ Identity and difference, unity and plurality, oneness and
manyness are thoroughly co-relative—joined in a dialectical relation of
reciprocal implication. This pluralized unity and unified plurality is the
ontological matrix of truth's relativity.

V. Symbolics of Relative Truth

Truth is the unity of thought and being, the coincidence of subjectivity and objectivity, the coadunation of sense and reference. From the perspective of relational ontology, however, this coalescence is not created by the conjunction of independent opposites, but is the self-conscious explication of radical (*radix*) unity. Our onto-noetic analysis suggests that truth is relative *because* meaning is contextual and being is relational. Or, as stated earlier, contextualized meaning and relational meaning join in relative truth disclosed through symbolic awareness.

Epistemological and semantic considerations suggest the perspectival relativity of truth. The historicity of consciousness establishes the inescapable situatedness of the knowing subject. Cognitive activity arises through the confluence of multiple conditioning factors, and issues in knowledge that inevitably bears the mark of the situation within which it is generated. Moreover, we have seen that meaning is contextual. Meaning remains unspecifiable apart from dialogic relation with alternative points of view. The synchronic and diachronic extensiveness of such relationality implies that meaning is inexhaustible and ever revisable. Consequently the meaningfulness of truth necessarily entails dialectical relation with contrasting frames of interpretation and is constantly subject to re-formation. Truth emerges only through the synchronic and diachronic interplay of truths. In sum, truth is relative to the perspective from which it is apprehended and is co-relative with implicated truths whose reciprocity it presupposes./23/

The relativity of the *ordo cognoscendi*, however, does not necessarily distort the *ordo essendi*. To the contrary, the relationality of being is inherently dialectical. In other words, that which thought seeks to grasp is itself relative. As a result of the sociality of being, determinate identity assumes concretion through internal relation with difference. Particular phenomena are posited by an extensive mutual interaction that forms a single complex web. Our ontological investigation has shown the synchronic and diachronic coordinates of constitutive relationality. Determinate identity is established through association with co-existing entities and through location within temporal process. Due to the historical unfolding of multiple ingredient relations, being is always in the process of becoming. Dynamic, dialectical actuality cannot be re-presented in static, sharply delineated categories of cognition. If such being is to be known, it must be grasped relative to otherness from which it is inseparable, and must be regularly reconstrued as it re-constructs. As an adequate reflection of the energetics of being, truth changes—it requires constant re-visioning./24/

Relative truth is the interface of contextual meaning and relational being which is most fully disclosed to symbolic awareness. Ray Hart points out that symbols "serve to carry over into consciousness the carrying over between things, and between things and the self, in their very being."

Symbolic consciousness "is the disposition of the mind as a whole to the 'thing' in plural presentiment to the intentionality of consciousness in its plurisignification" (247)./25/ The polysemy of symbols reveals the polymorphism of being. As Ricoeur maintains, "the sole philosophical interest in symbolism is that it reveals, by its structure of double meaning, the equivocalness of being: 'Being speaks in many ways.' Symbolism's raison d'être is to open the multiplicity of meaning to the equivocalness of being" (1974:67). The symbol mirrors the interplay of presence and absence, disclosure and concealment characteristic of determinate being. A symbol always means more than it says, and being is always more than it appears. Unfathomed relations remain hidden and unrealized potency lies dormant in all actuality. The density of constitutive relations and the nascence of concrete actuality engender a dissonance between manifest and latent content in the reflection of being in consciousness. The multivalence of symbols captures the multidimensionality of being in a way that establishes the need for a constant process of decipherment in which we reformulate our notions in order more fully to penetrate synchronic and diachronic relations that are ontologically definitive. By maintaining the tension between the revealed and the concealed, symbolic awareness insures that knowledge always evolves through ceaseless reinterpretation. For symbolic consciousness, truth, as being itself, forever be-comes. We may conclude with Brown:

> The letter killeth, but the spirit giveth life. Literal meanings as against spiritual or symbolical interpretations, a matter of Life against Death. The return to symbolism, the rediscovery that everything is symbolic—*alles Vergängliche nur ein Gleichniss.* . . .
>
> Everything is symbolic, everything is holy. There is no special time or place or person, privileged to represent the rest. And then democracy can begin. The many are made one when the totality is in every part. When one thing is taken up, all things are taken up with it; one flower is the spring. It is all there all the time. (191, 239)/26/

Describing the transition from "early modern" to "modern" religion, Robert Bellah argues that "The central feature of the change is the collapse of the dualism that was so crucial to all the historic religions." Bellah is quick to explain that "This is not to be interpreted as a return to primitive monism: it is not that a single world has replaced a double one but that an infinitely multiplex one has replaced the simple duplex structure. It is not that life has become again a 'one possibility thing' but that it has become an infinite possibility thing" (40). Such pluralization often leads to psychological, intellectual, and social fragmentation. The fundamental religious, philosophical, and existential issue facing our time is the perennial problem of the relation between oneness and manyness. How can we mediate unity and plurality within and without? Not infrequently psychosocial pluralization brings an acute awareness of perspectival relativism that results in the stilling of the theological and metaphysical impulse. Throughout this essay, we have attempted to overcome such paralysis and to render theological language hearable by exploring some of the metaphysical presuppositions and implications of relativism. The wedding of a relativistic epistemology and a relational ontology enables us to appreciate with Hegel that: "Appearance is the process of arising into being and passing away again, a process that itself does not arise and does not pass away, but is in itself, and constitutes reality and the life-movement of truth. The truth is thus the Bacchanalian revel, where not one member is sober; and because every member no sooner becomes detached than it *eo ipso* collapses straightway, the revel is just as much a state of transparent unbroken calm" (1967:105). Being *within* becoming; unity *within* plurality; identity *within* difference; truth *within* truths; constancy *within* change; peace *within* flux.

Notes

/1/   For an examination of major eighteenth and nineteenth century forces operative in the modification of the contemporary theological and philosophical imagination, see Taylor, 1977:185–235.

/2/   Proponents of the polytheistic position do not seem to realize that the complete pluralization of consciousness is the destruction of its human form. Human self-consciousness presupposes the simultaneous maintenance of plurality and unity. If unity does not accompany plurality, we cannot even be aware of plurality as plurality, and in the absence of any inner difference, we are unable to recognize our self-identity.

/3/   It might be argued that such a program is inherently self-contradictory. Rather than necessitating further metaphysical reflection, the recognition of perspectival relativism seems to render metaphysics impossible. This line of argument, however, artificially separates epistemology and ontology. Every epistemology (even a relativistic one) harbors an ontology. By disclosing the ontological presuppositions implicit in relativistic epistemology, we discover novel possibilities for theological reflection.

/4/   In light of the seemingly ineradicable ambiguity of the word "relativism," it might be argued that use of an alternative category would help to avoid unnecessary confusion. Despite the danger of misinterpretation, the term "relativism" continues to be well-suited for the purposes of this essay. We have already indicated that the argument of the paper seeks to address theological and religious problems that grow out of a relativistic view of human knowledge. Although the movement from strictly epistemological preoccupations to ontological questions casts a different light on the issue, the fundamental problematic remains closely tied to what recently has gone by the name "relativism." Secondly, and more importantly, the etymology of "relative" points to the conclusion toward which the argument moves. Strictly defined, "relative" means "having mutual relationship; related to, or connected with, each other; arising from depending on, or determined by, relation to something else or to each other" (*Oxford English Dictionary*). It derives from the Latin "*relativus*" meaning "having relation or reference to."

/5/   The extreme subjectivization of knowledge usually results from a view of the relationship between subject and object that is insufficiently dialectical. The position developed in this paper implies an understanding of the subject-object correlation which recognizes the inseparability of the creative contribution of the knowing subject and the persistent resistance of the known object. Overemphasis on either aspect of this dialectic leads to an inadequate epistemology. Elaboration and defense of this suggestion, however, would take us beyond the bounds of the present inquiry and thus must await a later essay. The general direction of the argument would follow the course identified in Hegel's effort to offer an alternative to the choice between what he regarded as subjective idealism and a simplistically empirical epistemology. Stated as concisely as possible, the situated locus of the knower is grounded in the nature of being-itself.

/6/   The usual understanding of relativity and absoluteness as mutually exclusive opposites makes these suggestions particularly puzzling, if not flatly contradictory. The plausibility of the position developed in this paper depends upon a reinterpretation of the relationship between identity and difference by means of a reexamination of the notion of negation. This is developed in the fourth section of the essay.

/7/   In this case, the phenomena represented are competing *Lebensanschauungen* or contending hermeneutical matrices. As our attention shifts from epistemological to ontological concerns, the phenomena involved become concrete actualities or imaginable possibilities.

/8/   In opposition to the insistence on the dialectical constitution of meaning, it might be argued that contextualization only works when one is dealing with two different perspectives of the same logical type governed by the same rules of inference. One could affirm that particular perspectives within a common conceptual grid define each other through mutual interrelationship, but deny that such definitive contextual relativity obtains for perspectives illustrative of different ordering frameworks that embody contrasting modes of reasoning. It would seem, however, that this objection is answerable in terms of the argument advanced to support the contextualization of meaning. Competing conceptual grids expressing discordant forms of reasoning, as well as various perspectives sharing fundamental logical assumptions define themselves through a reciprocity in which each becomes itself relative to an other. The distinctiveness of the principles of inference governing any hermeneutical screen emerge in contrast with alternative forms of reflection and judgment. Taken by itself, "primitive mentality" no more can know its primitiveness than "mature thought" by itself can recognize its maturity. The effort to drive apart different ordering frames without simultaneously establishing their inextricable relationship rests upon blindness to the identity that lies at the base of all difference.

/9/   Although much of the argument of the present essay draws heavily on the position of Hegel, this is one point at which Hegel's analysis must be supplemented by insights from Kierkegaard. From Kierkegaard's perspective, Hegel's position reduced temporal process to simple exfoliation of what was implicit from the beginning in a way that undercut any possibility of freedom, creativity, or novelty. In developing his critique of the Hegelian system, Kierkegaard emphasized the discontinuity between the outstanding future and the present past. Kierkegaard insisted that freedom and responsibility presuppose inbreaking futurity. For an elaboration of this point, see Taylor, 1975, esp. Chap. 3.

/10/   Pannenberg offers a helpful insight: "Of course every event has its particular character and meaning only within the nexus of events to which it belongs from the very beginning"(98).

/11/   It should be stressed that there is a structural homology between the negativity characteristic of the synchronic and diachronic axes. The details of this isomorphism will become apparent in the next section of the paper.

/12/   The same line of argument, of course, pertains to B''s relation to A'', C, and C''.

/13/   A musical analogy might help to clarify our argument at this point. As synchronic and diachronic coordinates intersect to form specific meaning, so harmony and melody join in musical composition.

/14/   Our effort to join synchronicity and diachronicity in the contextualization of meaning seeks to overcome the tension between structuralist and hermeneutical modes of interpretation. While structuralists tend to stress the synchronic axis, recent hermeneuticists are prone to focus on the diachronic axis. As our analysis suggests, thorough interpretation requires both factors. For a discussion of this problem, see Ricoeur, 1974:27–61.

/15/   The recognition of the relationality of being constituted by the interplay of identity and difference lies at the heart of the Christian doctrine of the trinity (*Dreieinigkeit*). According to the Christian definition, God is three-in-one and one-in-three—pluralized unity and unified plurality. Apart from such a dialectical interpretation of identity and difference, incarnational theology is impossible. One of the primary theological and philosophical puzzles confronting Church fathers who attempted to formulate the doctrine of the trinity was the articulation of a notion of unity that includes, rather than excludes plurality. Trinitarian theology walks the fine line between abstract monotheism and contradictory polytheism.

/16/   Emphasis added. It should be clear that the sublation of simple difference is not the abolition of distinction. Distinction remains as the ground of both identity and difference.

/17/   Our analysis of diachronicity suggests that the modalities of phenomenal presence are distinguishable. Present phenomena are actually on hand, while past and future phenomena are present as absent—the past as having been and the future as yet to be. The presence of the present is inseparable from the simultaneous presence and absence of past and future. Therefore it is an oversimplification to regard the present as merely present, for at the same time it is in itself absent. This point is developed in more detail in what follows.

/18/   This ontological insight might appear to pose problems for the interpretation of relativity presented in this paper. When relations are construed as internal, is there not an important sense in which nothing (no-thing) can be relative, since there is no-thing sufficiently itself to be qualified by relation to other? Does not the internality of relations dissolve the otherness upon which relativity depends? Such questions miss the point we have been pressing. It is assumed that the identity of determinate phenomena is constituted in itself, apart from relation to other. Relations thus remain secondary and external to pre-established identity. Any mitigation of the discreteness of determinate phenomena is regarded as an encroachment on individual identity that threatens the loss of concrete particularity. We have seen, however, that this position is self-negating. The very formation and maintenance of the in-itself is impossible apart from being-for-other. Existence-in-itself comes into being through the mediation of relation to otherness. Far from dissolving the otherness upon which relativity depends, relations form the determinacy without which otherness is impossible. In-itself and for-other, identity and difference, assertion and negation are inseparable. Nothing can be itself first and then come into relation with difference, for it becomes itself only through ingredient otherness.

/19/   A corollary of this suggestion is that permanence and change are not antithetical. Permanence is the unchangeability of change—the immutability of mutability. As unity and multiplicity are indissolubly joined, so permanence and change are indivisible. In more theological language, eternity is found in time, in history. God is incarnate.

/20/   With the recognition of the nature of relational ontology, some of the ethical implications of this line of analysis begin to emerge. The effort to acknowledge difference need not necessarily lead to an uncritical relativism that is finally indistinguishable from nihilism. Relationality suggests criteria such as comprehensiveness, inclusiveness, and coherence by which normative discriminations can be made and through which a critical relativism can be developed. The formulation of the ethical correlate of the epistemological and ontological position developed in this paper is the task of another essay.

/21/   This structure of relationality qualifies for what usually goes by the name "Being-itself" or "Being-in-general." Unlike such abstractions, relation is inseparable from relata. We can now see more clearly that what remains constant amid relativity is constitutive relationality, interpreted in terms of the structure of double negativity. Perduring relations form the ground of being of determinate phenomena by establishing particular entities in their definitive co-relativity. Thoroughgoing relativism is impossible apart from the absoluteness of relationality. It might be helpful to recall an earlier theological expression of this point. God and world cannot exist apart from one another. God forever becomes incarnate, and the finite is always in the process of becoming reconciled with the infinite.

/22/   It is important to recognize that by describing the whole as the structure of relation through which parts are constituted, rather than viewing the whole as the sum total of the parts, this position avoids a hermeneutical impasse. It is not necessary to know everything (i.e., every particular phenomenon) in order to know anything. Put differently, knowledge is possible before the end of history, for history is always finishing, though ever refinishing.

/23/   Truth-itself (as Being-itself) is an empty abstraction. Definable truth assumes determinate form that grows out of dialectical interrelation with otherness.

/24/   Pannenberg correctly contends that "Every absolutization of a contemporary truth would at once misunderstand the historical multiplicity of pictures of the truth. In this situation, unity of truth can now only be thought of as the history of truth, meaning in effect that truth itself has a history and that its essence is the process of this history. Historical change itself must be thought of as the essence of truth if its unity is still to be maintained without narrow-mindedly substituting a particular perspective for the whole truth. To date, Hegel's system should be regarded as the most significant attempt at a solution to this problem. It is distinguished from other philosophies of history by the fact that truth is not to be found already existing somewhere as a finished product, but is instead thought of as history as process" (20–21).

/25/   Hart makes these remarks in the context of his extraordinarily insightful exploration of the imagination. What I have labeled "symbolic awareness" bears many similarities to Hart's "imagination."

/26/   Compare: "In the last analysis, Goethe's statement 'Everything is a symbol' is the most comprehensive formulation of the hermeneutical idea. It means that everything points to another thing. . . . But the statement implies something else as well: nothing comes forth in the one meaning that is simply offered to us. The impossibility of surveying all relations is just as much present in Goethe's concept of the symbolic as is the vicarious function of the particular for the presentation of the whole" (Gadamer:103).

Works Consulted

Altizer, T. J. J.
    1977   *The Self-Embodiment of God.* New York: Harper & Row.

Bellah, R. N.
    1970   *Beyond Belief: Essays on Religion in a Post Traditional World.* New York: Harper & Row.

Berger, Peter
    1974   *The Homeless Mind: Modernization and Consciousness.* New York: Random House.

Brown, N. O.
    1968   *Love's Body.* New York: Random House.

Crites, Stephen
    1975   "Angels We Have Heard," *Religion as Story.* Ed. J. B. Wiggins. New York: Harper & Row.

Gadamer, H. G.
1976   *Philosophical Hermeneutics*, Ed. D. E. Linge. Berkeley: University of California Press.

Gouldner, A. W.
1965   "Anti-Minotaur: The Myth of Value-Free Sociology," *Sociology on Trial*. Eds. M. Stein and A. Vidich. Englewood Cliffs: Prentice-Hall, Inc.

Hart, R. L.
1968   *Unfinished Man and the Imagination*. New York: Herder and Herder.

Harvey, V. A.
1972   *The Historian and the Believer: The Morality of Historical Knowledge and Christian Belief*. New York: Macmillan Co.

Hegel, G. W. F
1967   *The Phenomenology of Mind*. Trans. J. Baillie. New York: Harper & Row.
1969   *Science of Logic*. Trans. A. V. Miller. New York: Humanities Press.

Hyppolite, Jean
1974   *Genesis and Structure of Hegel's Phenomenology of Spirit*. Trans. S. Cherniak and J. Heckman. Evanston: Northwestern University Press.

Kaufman, G. D.
1960   *Relativism, Knowledge and Faith*. Chicago: University of Chicago Press.

Kermode, Frank
1975   *The Sense of An Ending: Studies in the Theory of Fiction*. New York: Oxford University Press.

Little, H. G.
1974   *Decision and Responsibility: A Wrinkle in Time*. Missoula, MT: Scholars Press.

Merleau-Ponty, Maurice
1966   *Phenomenology of Perception*. London: Routledge and Kegan Paul, Ltd.

Miller, David
1974   *The New Polytheism: Rebirth of the Gods and Goddesses*. New York: Harper & Row.

Niebuhr, R. R.
1972   *Experiential Religion*. New York: Harper & Row.

Ogilvy, J.
1977   *Many Dimensional Man: Decentralizing Self, Society and the Sacred*. New York: Oxford University Press.

Pannenberg, Wolfhart
1971   *Basic Questions in Theology*, vol. I. Trans. F. H. Kehm.
            Philadelphia: Fortress Press.

Ricoeur, Paul
1970   *Freud and Philosophy: An Essay on Interpretation*. Trans. D.
            Savage. New Haven: Yale University Press.
1973   "Creativity in Language: Word, Polysemy, Metaphor." *Philosophy Today*, 17:97–111.
1974   *The Conflict of Interpretations: Essays in Hermeneutics*. Ed.
            D. Ihde. Evanston: Northwestern University Press.

Stevens, Wallace
1957   *Opus Posthumous*. Ed. S. F. Morse. New York: Alfred A.
            Knopf.

Taylor, M. C.
1975   *Kierkegaard's Pseudonymous Authorship: A Study of Time
            and the Self*. Princeton: Princeton University Press.
1977   *Religion and the Human Image*. Englewood Cliffs: Prentice-
            Hall, Inc.

Wilson, Bryan
1974   *Rationality*. London: Blackwell.

Interpreting Interpretation

The art object is a potency, a call on imagination (that of the collaborating appreciator) produced by imagination (that of the artist), a thing inducing the movement of activated imagination in a certain tendency. But the art object *qua* stable existent is a merely necessary, not a sufficient condition for the emergent being of the work of art. The art object is not a sufficient condition because it does not possess in itself the makings of the whole, the completed work of art. Hegel grasped this point when he said that the art object " . . . is . . . not by itself an animating thing; it is a whole only when its process of coming to be is taken along with it." The art object takes its process of coming to be along with it only as the collaborating, co-operating, answering imagination of its perceiver is thrown into act. The emergent work of art therefore depends upon aesthetic experience that " . . . is a creative act of the same order as the act of artistic creation."

Ray L. Hart

I. The Strange and Self-Estrangement

Hermes, the discoverer of language and writing, is the messenger of the gods, the one who presents the Other. Hermeneutics, the art of interpretation, arises from the encounter with difference—meeting the other, the alien, the strange. The voice of the other *demands* interpretation. "To 'make one's own' what was previously 'foreign,'" avers Ricoeur, "remains the ultimate aim of all hermeneutics" (1976:91). If, however, the strange is to be hearable, if interpretation is to be both possible and necessary, otherness cannot simply be other, difference not merely different. The Word must become flesh and dwell among us. That which calls for interpretation must be strange enough to require decipherment, yet familiar enough to permit it. Hermeneutics, in other words, presupposes an interplay of the familiar and the strange, a reciprocity of identity and difference in which each becomes itself through dialectical relation to the other. Conversation with the other renders the strange familiar and the familiar strange. It is precisely this identity-within-difference that makes the encounter with the alien self-alienating. Interpretation is always an adventure, a journey (*ventura*) to (*ad*) the other. Seeing with the other forces one to see oneself *other*-wise. If meeting the alien is not to remain self-alienating, this journey has to become an odyssey. Enriched by his sojourn, the prodigal must return to grasp the familiar anew. Through the activity of journey and return, the self discovers *itself* in otherness. Interpretation, therefore, is a *social* process. So conceived, hermeneutics is not merely the effort to comprehend the strange; it is also the struggle to overcome estrangement.

II. Tradition and Task

Though the roots of hermeneutics lie deeply buried in the traditions of Greek philosophical reflection and Judaeo-Christian scriptural interpretation, the modern discussion of the issue was initiated by Schleiermacher in his classic work entitled *Hermeneutik*. In an effort to respond to Enlightenment critiques of religious belief and practice, Schleiermacher develops a *general* hermeneutics in which he attempts to define clearly the principles of valid textual interpretation./1/ Profoundly influenced by the romantic recovery of the significance of unique individuality and veneration of creative genius, Schleiermacher regards interpretation as a process of reconstruction. By attempting to place himself within the mental frame of the author, the interpreter seeks to recreate the creative act through which the text first emerged. As Gadamer points out, Schleiermacher believes understanding to be "the reproduction of an original production"(263). Reconstruction, however, is not simple repetition, for something novel emerges through this interpretive process. The perspective of the interpreter affords an angle of vision from which he can understand the author better than the author understood himself.

It should be evident that for Schleiermacher the text is essentially an expression—the written word is the externalization or objectification of the intention of the author./2/ Consequently, the text cannot be understood apart from the intentionality which called it into being and which it continues to embody. As a matter of fact, authorial intention is, for Schleiermacher, the norm for interpretation./3/ Without an intuitive understanding of the author or a divinatory identification of interpreter and author, the text cannot be grasped properly. Since Schleiermacher is sensitive to the inextricable relationship between self and world, he insists that comprehending the creative intention of the author presupposes understanding the world from which the work arose and to which it was addressed. The interpretive process, therefore, involves the psychological and historical transposition of the interpreter into the mind and world of the author. This imaginative leap is supposed to allow one to attend the labor of work aborning. To the eyes of such an attendant, Schleiermacher contends, meaning is transparent.

Schleiermacher's extraordinarily influential theory of interpretation lately has come under attack from two contrasting points of view: structuralism and hermeneutics, *sensu strictissimo*./4/ Although these two schools of interpretation differ significantly, they both insist that the hermeneutics of romanticism, illustrated by Schleiermacher, falls prey to what W. K. Wimsatt has labeled "the intentional fallacy." Recovery of the subjective intention of the author, Wimsatt argues, is neither possible nor desirable. Preoccupation with creative purpose diverts attention from the proper object of interpretation—the text itself.

In order to depsychologize and dehistoricize interpretation, structuralists, guided by insights garnered from linguists such as Saussure, attempt to pose an alternative to reconstructive hermeneutics. For the structuralist, interpretation is "carried out without explicit reference to the subject" (Culler:81)./5/ Roland Barthes goes so far as to suggest that "as an institution, the author is dead: his civil status, his biographical person have disappeared; disposed, they no longer exercise over his work the formidable paternity whose account literary history, teaching, and public opinion had the responsibility of establishing and renewing" (1975:27)./6/ Having broken the tyrannical "reign of the Author," the interpreter seeks "to define the principles of structuration that operate not only through individual works but through the relationships among works over the whole field of literature" (Scholes:10). The interpreter, in other words, no longer reads the text in terms of the idiosyncratic intentions of the author, but tries to discern universal structures, categories, functions, and codes within the text itself. Robert Scholes explains: "At the heart of the idea of structuralism is the idea of system: a complete, self-regulating entity that adapts to new conditions by transforming its features while retaining its systematic structure. Every literary unit from the individual sentence to the whole order of words can be seen in relation to the concept of system. In particular, we can look at individual works, literary genres, and the whole of literature as related systems, and at literature as a system within the larger system of human culture. The relationships that obtain between any of these systematic units may be studied, and that study will be, in some sense, structuralist" (10).

As the antithesis of romantic hermeneutics, structuralism errs in the opposite direction by committing what Ricoeur describes as "the fallacy of the absolute text." In reaction to the problematic implications of the intentional fallacy, the structuralist makes the mistake of "hypostasizing the text as an authorless entity." He continues: "If the intentional fallacy overlooks the semantic autonomy of the text, the opposite fallacy forgets that the text remains a discourse told by somebody, said by someone else about something" (Ricoeur, 1976:30). Doubtless it is necessary to correct the implicit reductionism of the romantic theory of interpretation by underscoring the "semantic autonomy of the text." But the independence and the integrity of the object of interpretation cannot be allowed to obscure the expressive character of the creative process, or to distort the intentional nature of the work of art.

Recent hermeneutical theories which have grown out of Heidegger's recognition of the intrinsic temporality of human existence tend to support the efforts of structuralists to depsychologize interpretation. Hans-Georg Gadamer, a leader of this school of thought, repeatedly insists that "texts do not ask to be understood as a living expression of the subjectivity of their writers" (356). The historicity of consciousness makes it impossible to understand the other (either present or past) as the other understands (or understood) himself. Even were such comprehension possible, Gadamer maintains, it would not really disclose textual meaning. It is uncertain whether what is obtained through historical reconstruction "is really what we look for as the meaning of the work of art, and whether it is correct to see understanding as a second creation, the reproduction of the original production. Ultimately, this view of hermeneutics is as foolish as all restitution and restoration of past life. The reconstruction of the original circumstances, like all restoration is a pointless undertaking in view of the historicity of our being" (148–49).

To depsychologize interpretation, however, is not necessarily to dehistoricize understanding. To the contrary, temporal beings can understand *only* historically. Hermeneuticists, therefore, are critical of the structuralist emphasis on synchronicity to the virtual exclusion of diachronicity, and are suspicious of preoccupation with seemingly atemporal universals at the apparent expense of eventual individuality./7/ According to this line of argument, any adequate theory of interpretation must recognize the correlative historicity of consciousness and incompleteness of the text. Both the subject interpreting and the object interpreted are, in Hart's terms, "unfinished."

The rehistoricization of interpretation does not inevitably entangle hermeneutics in the dilemmas encountered by romanticism. In place of Schleiermacher's "archaeological" hermeneutics in which the text is understood in terms of the world from which it originated, Gadamer proposes a "teleological" hermeneutics in which the text is interpreted in terms of the world it projects./8/ Since the text is not to be viewed as an objectification of individual subjectivity, "to understand it does not mean primarily to reason one's way back into the past, but to have a present involvement in what is said" (353). Meaning is not the function of the relationship of expression to authorial intention, but emerges from the encounter between text and interpreter which is mediated by historical tradition. The horizon of experience projected in the text fuses with the horizon of the interpreter's own experience in a way that simultaneously uncovers personal prejudice (*Vorurteil*) and reveals novel experiential possibilities. *Horizontverschmelzung* is *Horizontausdehnung*. As the interpreter questions the text, the text questions the interpreter. Through this dialectical relationship, subject (interpreter) and object (text) assume determinate identity and become themselves. Consequently, the process of interpretation is intrinsic to both subject and object. This insight, Gadamer maintains, corrects a fundamental error of post-Cartesian philosophy that has been perpetuated by the inordinate veneration of scientific methodology. No longer is it possible to view subjectivity and objectivity as fundamentally antithetical, and correlatively to regard interpretation as the activity in which a self-contained subject seeks to penetrate an object which possesses being-in-itself. Gadamer believes that relation is more primordial than bifurcation./9/ Subject and object, interpreter and text are incomplete apart from one another. Gadamer explains that "the work of art is not an object that stands over against a subject for itself. Instead the work of art has its true being in the fact that it becomes an experience changing the person experiencing it" (92). Interpretation, therefore, is the process through which the text becomes itself and the interpreter becomes himself./10/

It is important to stress that in his effort to develop a hermeneutics that does justice to the historicity of consciousness, Gadamer places primary emphasis upon the relationship between transmitted text and subsequent interpreter, rather than on the connection between original utterance and antecedent utterer. For Gadamer, as for Heidegger, human being is essentially futural. By projecting a new horizon of possible experience, the text discloses a future into which the individual can freely move through the activity of appropriation. To understand the text, it is necessary to apply it to oneself. Interpretation, in other words, is inseparable from application. In the interpretive process, the text presents itself anew and the interpreter undergoes personal transformation. Gadamer's long and involved argument rests upon the conviction that interpretation involves a *creative* interaction of subject and object.

All of the theories we have discussed briefly contribute significantly to our understanding of the complex activity of interpretation./11/ And yet each point of view taken by itself seems incomplete and thus inadequate. Schleiermacher's romantic hermeneutics is so concerned with beginnings that it fails to hear the ongoing address of the text. The structuralist stress on synchronic form too often overlooks the importance of the diachronic process. Finally, Gadamer's teleological hermeneutics remains curiously insensitive to the historical origin of the text. The shortcomings of these alternative analyses become evident when it is recognized that each theory of interpretation focuses primarily on *one* of the three temporal ecstases. Schleiermacher views the text in terms of the past from which it emerged; structuralists seek to discern presently abiding structures; and Gadamer is concerned to discover the future which the text opens./12/ But as Heidegger and before him Kierkegaard have shown, in human existence temporal ecstases are not discrete, but overlap, interpenetrate, and mutually condition one another. Since interpretation is a human activity, an adequate hermeneutics must take into account all dimensions of temporality. The significant differences separating romanticists, structuralists, and hermeneuticists, however, render impossible any simple combination of their insights. In order to arrive at a satisfactory theory of interpretation, it is necessary to reexamine the relation of author, text, and interpreter. Toward this end, we shall turn our attention to the closely related problems of work and the work of art.

III. Work

"Work" is both a noun and a verb. One works to produce a work. The work of art, for example, is at once *l'objet d'art* and the process through which this object is formed. The polysemy of the work "work" suggests the inseparability of production and product. The creative subject and the created object are bound in a dialectical relation of mutual constitution. The essential sociality of the labor process, therefore, is reflected and embodied in the labor product. No one has done more to elucidate the intricate dynamics of work than Hegel. Hegel's analysis of labor, of course, forms the philosophical foundation of Marxism. While Marxist thinkers have expanded and deepened important aspects of Hegel's point of view, their particular theoretical commitments and practical interests have obscured the broader implications of his argument. A reconsideration of Hegel's understanding of work can shed significant light on the process of interpretation.

The *locus classicus* of Hegel's analysis of labor is his examination of the master-slave relation in the second chapter of the *Phenomenology of Spirit*. Although this section of Hegel's work is one of the most frequently discussed texts in the history of philosophy, commentators rarely probe the connection between the master-slave dialectic and the purpose and course of Hegel's overall analysis of the experience of consciousness. In the *Phenomenology*, Hegel sets himself the twofold task of describing the incremental reintegration of subjectivity and objectivity and of exploring the internal relations definitive of specific objects and the interrelations constitutive of particular subjects. Hegel's concern with these correlative issues is especially evident in the first three chapters of his argument. By means of a careful investigation of consciousness, self-consciousness, and reason, Hegel attempts to demonstrate the sublation of the apparent opposition of subject and object in cognitive reflection and volitional action. On the one hand, through the coimplicated processes of sense-intuition, perception, and understanding, the knowing subject discovers itself in the known object. Consciousness of objects reveals itself to be the self-consciousness of the subject. Self-consciousness, on the other hand, necessarily involves consciousness of the self as object. Put differently, self-consciousness is impossible apart from self-objectification. While consciousness entails the subjectification of objectivity, self-consciousness implies the objectification of subjectivity. Reason, for Hegel, is the dialectical union of consciousness and self-consciousness through which subject and object join to form an identity-within-difference. Hegel's consideration of work plays a crucial role in the progression of his argument. The labor process discloses the implications of the initial emergence of *Geist* in the struggle for recognition and points toward the eventual realization of spirit in practical reason./13/

Hegel maintains that while consciousness begins with a belief in the essentiality of the object and the inessentiality of the subject, self-consciousness initially assumes the essentiality of the subject and the inessentiality of the object. Throughout the circuitous course of its education (*Bildung*), self-consciousness attempts to achieve satisfaction by giving objective expression to its subjective certainty. The most primitive form of self-consciousness is desire. The desiring subject seeks to assert its own substantiality and independence, and to establish the insubstantiality and dependence of that which opposes it by negating its object. "Certain of the nothingness of this other, it explicitly affirms that this nothingness is *for it* the truth of the other; it destroys the independent object and thereby gives itself the certainty of itself as a *true* certainty, a certainty that has become explicit for self-consciousness itself *in an objective manner*" (109; 139)./14/ Desire, however, is always frustrated and inevitably fails to achieve complete satisfaction. It is insatiable, perpetually requiring another object through whose negation it can assert itself. Furthermore, such intended self-affirmation is actually self-negation. In quest of fulfillment, the desiring subject annuls its self-sufficiency and demonstrates its reliance upon the object of desire. The once seemingly dependent object now appears to be independent of the subject. In light of this independence, Hegel concludes that self-consciousness "can achieve satisfaction only when the object itself effects the negation within itself" (109; 139). The *self*-negation of the other upon which the truth of self-consciousness depends can be brought about solely by a self-conscious being. In other words, "*Self-consciousness achieves its satisfaction only in another self-consciousness*" (110; 139). This insight forms an essential link in Hegel's phenomenological analysis.

"Self-consciousness," Hegel argues, "exists in and for itself when, and by the fact that, it so exists for another; that is, it exists only in being recognized" (111; 141). In order to establish the objective truth of its subjective certainty, a self-conscious subject must confront another self-conscious agent and win from that other the acknowledgment of the subject's own substantiality and independence. The recognition granted by the other presupposes the other's self-negation as an autonomous individual. Since the other is also a self-conscious being, however, he is an equal partner in the struggle for recognition, and seeks the same acknowledgment from the subject confronting him. Consequently, the endeavor of each self-conscious subject to affirm itself by exacting the self-negation of its other involves the effort to accomplish the negation of its own negation. In the language of speculative logic, subjects are bound together in an internal relation of double negativity. "Each is for the other the mean, through which each mediates itself with itself and unites with itself; and each is for itself, and for the other, an immediate being on its own account, which at the same time is such only through mediation. They *recognize* themselves as mutually recognizing one another" (112; 143). Each subject becomes itself through relation to the other, and hence includes the other within it as constitutive of its own being. According to Hegel, the relationship of double negativity which sustains identity-within-difference is the essential structure of spirit. Self-consciousness's struggle for recognition, therefore, discloses the intersubjectivity of selfhood definitive of genuine spirit. Hegel maintains: "with this, we already have before us the notion of *spirit*. What still lies ahead is for consciousness to experience what spirit is— this absolute substance which is the unity of the different independent self-consciousnesses which, in their opposition enjoy perfect freedom and independence: 'I' that is 'we' and 'we' that is 'I'" (110; 140)./15/

It is obvious, however, that if carried to completion, the struggle for recognition is self-destructive. Realizing that self-consciousness presupposes life, one contestant concedes the recognition sought by the other. By so doing, the vanquished subject (*sub-jectum*) becomes a slave, and the victor the lord and master. Apparently the master has established the truth of his own independence, or his being for self. Correlatively, the slave seems to be completely dependent upon the master, or merely to possess being for another. But, as always, appearances are deceptive. Since one can be a master only in relation to a slave, the master is dependent upon the slave for his mastery, and the slave is, in fact, master of the master. The lord *needs* the obedient acknowledgment and servile labor of his bondsman. In himself, the master is a slave—a slave to his own slave. Initially the bondsman is unaware of his implicit mastery. In the face of the omnipotent lord, the servant is gripped by fear and trembling and believes himself absolutely dependent upon the fortuitous grace of the other. For Hegel, this "fear of the lord is indeed the beginning of wisdom" (117–18; 148). Having confronted its own nothingness, servile consciousness "has trembled in every fibre of its being, and everything solid and stable has been shaken to its foundations. But this pure universal movement, the absolute melting-away of everything stable, is the simple essence of self-consciousness, absolute negativity, *pure being-for-self*, which consequently is implicit in this consciousness" (117; 148). As the seemingly independent master is inherently for another, so the ostensibly dependent slave is essentially for self.

The bondsman becomes aware of his independence through the discipline of labor. Unlike desire, work is not the thoroughgoing negation of objectivity, but is the subject's transformation of the object into its own self-image. The product of labor is the objectification of the self. Work, Hegel argues, "is desire held in check, fleetingness staved off; in other words, work forms and shapes the thing. The negative relation to the object becomes its *form* and something *permanent*, because it is precisely for the worker that the object has independence. This *negative* middle term of the formative *activity* is at the same time the individuality or pure being-for-self of consciousness which now, in the work outside of it, acquires an element of permanance. Thus working consciousness comes to see the independent being [of the object] as its *own* independence" (118; 148)./16/ In labor, the self creates itself by giving birth to other. The subject alienates itself from itself by positing itself as an object, and returns to itself by discovering self in thing. Such self-relation in otherness forms the reconciliation of subject and object which is definitive of reason.

The true proportions of work only emerge with the recognition of the intersubjectivity of practical reason. The active self simultaneously sublates the antithesis of subjectivity and objectivity and overcomes opposition among particular agents. When poised for action, the subject faces objective reality which represents the potential for the subject's own self-realization. In Hegel's terms, objectivity is the in-itself of subjectivity. This is manifest in the interest the object evokes in the subject. The subject, conversely, is the in-itself of the object. This becomes evident in the subject's action on the object. In practical activity, the subject expresses itself in actuality in such a way that it also discloses the essence of the object by uncovering its latent potential. Subject and object join in a relation of reciprocal self-revelation in which their implicit identity-within-difference becomes explicit.

To secure this point, Hegel expands his account of the labor process to form an interpretation of practical activity in terms of three dialectically related moments. Subjective purpose is the abstract moment of indeterminate intention (universality). Purpose is realized (i.e., made real) by means of efficacious effort in which general intention assumes specific expression (particularity). The third moment closes the circle of action by recognizing purpose accomplished and intention embodied (individuality or concrete universality). At this point, the subject realizes its unity with the object by self-consciously comprehending objectivity as the objectification of its own subjectivity. So understood, practical activity is a process of double negation in which the subject negates its abstract indeterminacy by expressing itself in the object, and then negates this negation by reappropriating the other as itself.

It is important to recognize that the bond joining the active subject and its determinate expression in specific action is not a simple identification, but forms a differentiated unity which preserves distinction. "The work produced," Hegel contends, "is the reality which consciousness gives itself; it is that in which the individual is explicitly or for himself what he is implicitly or *in himself*, and in such a manner that the consciousness, for which the individual becomes explicit in the work, is not the particular, but the *universal* consciousness. In his work, he has placed himself altogether in the element of universality, in the qualityless void of being. The consciousness which withdraws from its work is, in fact, the universal consciousness in contrast to its work, which is *determinate* or *particular*—and it is universal because it is *absolute negativity* or action in this opposition. Thus it goes beyond itself in the work, and is itself the qualityless void which is left unfilled by its work" (242–43; 290–91). The self is not merely this, or any other single concretion. As an active agent, the subject is immanent in, though distinguishable from, the determinations predicated of it. Therefore, while Hegel admits that the work is the expression of the actor, he insists that the subject also differentiates itself from the objectivity with which it identifies.

The distinction of the subject from the product of its activity becomes clearer with the recognition that the self's self-objectification necessarily involves its being for others. The self can be for itself only insofar as it is for others. Hegel stresses that "the work [i.e., the subject's self-objectification] *is*; that is, it exists for other individualities, and is for them an alien actuality, which they must replace by their own in order to obtain through *their* action the consciousness of *their* unity with actuality; in other words, *their* interest in the work which stems from *their* original nature, is something different from this work's *own* peculiar interest, which is thereby converted into something different" (243; 291). Action elicits counteraction. Work becomes independent of worker and presents itself to other agents as an occasion for action by establishing a possibility in response to which they can realize themselves. The object produced by the subject's labor harbors potentiality that *necessarily* remains unrealized by the acting subject. The work is finished through the activity of responsive agents. The reaction of others to the product of labor is not extrinsic or accidental, but is intrinsic to the object itself. Since the object transcends its original creator and is completed through the activity of others, the product produces the producer as much as the producer produces the product. Because the identity of the worker is inseparable from an object whose determinateness is partly constituted by other actors, the creative subject is inherently a social being. Relation to other is mediate self-relation. Hence *both* subject *and* object emerge through creative labor.

Hegel defines corporate practical activity with the multivalent term *die Sache selbst*. Although usually translated "the fact of the matter," "the thing itself," or "the matter at hand," Royce's use of "cause" is a more accurate rendering of this problematic category./17/ Since Hegel conceives practical reason as universal (*allgemein*), his meaning can be better expressed by the term "common cause."/18/ The common cause is the joint activity of a community of subjects through which determinate objects are created and in which active participants assume unique individuality. The nature of the common cause, Hegel maintains, is "such that its *being* is the *action* of the single individual and of all individuals and whose action is immediately *for others*, or is a cause . . . only as the action of *each* and *all*: the essence which is the essence of all beings—the spiritual essence [*das geistige Wesen*]" (251–52; 300)./19/ In other words, *die Sache selbst* is "substance permeated by individuality; the *subject* in which there is individuality just as much *qua* individual, or *qua this particular* individual, as *qua all* individuals; and it is the universal which has being only as this action of all and each, and [is] an actuality through the fact that *this particular* consciousness knows it to be its own individual actuality and the actuality of all" (252; 300). As the work of each and all, the common cause is the creatrix of subject and object—it is the social process that is the ultimate ground of all that is.

Hegel's interpretation of work culminates in his detailed analysis of practical reason. Having originally set out from the perspective of natural consciousness in which a particular subject, isolated from all other particular subjects, confronts an alien object, separated from all other objects, Hegel gradually discloses the thoroughly dialectical relation of subjectivity and objectivity, as well as the internal relations among objects and the intersubjectivity of selfhood. The pivot upon which the argument turns is the understanding of labor. For Hegel, worker and work, regarded as both activity (verb) and artifact (noun), are complex social processes.

IV. Work of Art

Poesy alone can tell her dreams,
With the fine spell of words alone can save
Imagination from the sable charm
And dumb enchantment. Who alive can say
"Thou art no Poet—mayst not tell they dreams?"
Since every man whose soul is not a clod
Hath visions, and would speak, if he had loved
And been well nurtured in his mother tongue./20/

Ray Hart comments: "It is one of the cardinal functions of the work of art to create the creator; to correlate artistic genius and appreciative taste; in Kant's words, to arouse the man of taste 'to a feeling of his own originality'" (260). In order to grasp the significance of Hart's remark, we must unravel and reweave the intricate relation of artist, work, and interpreter./21/ Our analysis will be guided by Hegel's provocative account of work.

On the most basic level, the work of art is the expression of the author's intention. Artistic labor brings to birth an object which is the objectification of authorial purpose. Such intentionality, of course, is not merely conscious. The artist always plays on registers of which he is not fully aware. The notion of the work of art as an intentional object, therefore, must expand to encompass the multiple forces which converge upon, and the complex systems which operate through, the author. The artist's conscious intention is perpetually modulated by his personal and collective unconscious. Moreover, artistic creativity is conditioned by historical, social, and cultural factors which simultaneously inform and transcend the individual subject./22/ Given these insights, we are able to see that a *world* comes to expression in the work of art. The world thematized in the text inevitably reflects the psychological, social, cultural, and historical world within which the artist labors. In this sense, the art object takes its process of coming to be along with it—work (noun) incarnates work (verb). The dialectical relation between creative production and created product implies that the comprehension of *l'objet d'art* presupposes an understanding of the world in which it arises./23/ Archaeologists from Schleiermacher to Freud, therefore, have properly insisted that interpretation always involves reconstruction of intentional activity and historical circumstance. Though the historicity of consciousness admittedly makes it impossible to identify completely with the other, re-search can, nonetheless, unearth significant facets of conscious purpose and unconscious intention which originally called forth, and continue to be objectified in, the work of art.

The insistence on the importance of historical, social, cultural, and psychological reconstruction does not necessarily imply a reductive hermeneutics, and hence does not inevitably lead to the intentional fallacy. Hegel's consideration of labor demonstrates that self-objectification in work is at the same time self-alienation. Expression involves a distanciation through which the familiar becomes strange. Though the self expresses *itself* in work, the work ineluctably confronts its creator as other. "It is not," notes Barthes, "that the Author may not 'come back' in the Text, in his text, but he then does so as a 'guest'" (1977:161). The text, in other words, is not only dependent upon, but also becomes independent of the author. It assumes a life of its own. Louis Mackey goes so far as to argue: "The speech of a poet does not utter his inner states, but rather builds meanings into a free standing structure of language. Paradox, self-concealment, plural connotations, distentions of metaphor and the like are the shears by which he clips the umbilical of his fancy's child and sends it out on its own. His art is not the externalizing of himself, but the objectifying of a work of words: *poiesis*. What the poet produces is a verbal object (*poiema*) in which meanings, released from any personal interest he may vest in them, are neither affirmed nor denied, but simply placed. A poem in this sense does not *mean*—it does not urge the feelings and opinions of the poet on the reader. It *is*—as a thing made it is self-sufficient (*perfectum*) and bears no message not indigenous to its perfection" (284–85)./24/

The independence of work from author establishes the "semantic autonomy of the text" and provides partial justification for approaching the text as an "authorless entity." The methodological bracketing of authorial intention can disclose dimensions of the work which otherwise tend to go unnoticed. For instance, through a structural analysis of texts, it is possible to uncover latent codes which order the work and which, unbeknown to the author, inform creative activity. Too often, however, structuralists are insufficiently dialectical when they consider the author-text relation. The work of Lévi-Strauss suggests that intentional and structural analyses need not be mutually exclusive./25/ Upon the basis of deep structures universally exhibited in a variety of particular texts, Lévi-Strauss postulates the isomorphism of the creative subject and the created object. If one grants this homology, it can be argued that the examination of a text is also an exploration of the structure of the author's active subjectivity./26/

While granting the importance of acknowledging the semantic autonomy of the text, it must be stressed that this point of view easily leads to the mistaken apprehension of the object of art as a self-contained thing-in-itself. Hegel's account of work helps us to avoid this problematic conclusion by disclosing both the incompleteness and the relational character of the labor product. The work of art, like the artist himself, remains "unfinished." Rather than a finished product, the object is an on-going process—a historical event. As Hart points out, "the art object *qua* stable existent is a merely necessary, not a sufficient condition for the emergent being of the work of art. The art object is not a sufficient condition because it does not possess in itself the makings of the whole, the completed work of art. . . . The art object takes its process of coming to be along with it only as the collaborating, cooperating, answering imagination of its perceiver is thrown into act" (259). In artistic work, as in the labor process, action provokes reaction. The text which has become independent of the author addresses others and commands response. Creative response to the work of art is an essential aspect of all interpretation.

Apprehension of the art object involves the effort to appropriate the other, to familiarize the strange, through a process of interpretation. The activity of interpretation reenacts the Hegelian dialectic of desire/27/ which leads to the struggle for recognition and culminates in corporate practical activity. In his work the artist projects a horizon of experience which initially confronts other individuals as an alien reality to which they must respond. Ricoeur explains that the text offers "a new way of looking at things" or presents "an injunction to think in a certain manner. . . . The text speaks of a possible world and of a possible way of orienting oneself within it. The dimensions of the world are opened and disclosed by the text" (1976:88). One enters the world of the text through a process that Gadamer aptly labels the "fusion of horizons." Text and interpreter join to form a dialogical relationship which is mutually transformative./28/ To understand the text is to understand oneself in the text—to imagine oneself a member of the world the work projects. To see, in other words, is to see *with*. From this point of view, it becomes apparent that appreciation of a work of art is nothing less than an ecstatic (ἔκστασις) experience. The Word calls one to stand outside oneself in order to see all anew. Gadamer explains that "inasmuch as we encounter the work of art in the world and a world in the individual work of art, this does not remain a strange universe into which we are magically transported for a time. Rather, we learn to understand ourselves in it, and that means that we preserve the discontinuity of the experience in the continuity of our existence" (86). Genuine dialogue with the text simultaneously disorients and reorients the interlocutor. Through interpretation, one enters a new world in which the strange becomes familiar and the familiar becomes strange. "Here showing is at the same time creating a new mode of being" (Ricoeur, 1976:88). Thought and being join in *metanoia*, an ontological transformation wrought by creative re-visioning. With the recognition of self in text, the mere otherness of the work of art is sublated, and relation to the strange becomes a dimension of self-relation requisite for self-realization. By responding to the work of art,

the interpreter becomes *himself*. The act of interpretation, like the struggle
for recognition, leads to a self-understanding of otherness which reconciles
self and other and points toward the final negation of estrangement.

The consideration of the relation between text and interpreter must not,
however, obscure the implications of the process of interpretation for the art
object. Interpretation is not extrinsic to the work of art—a superfluous addition to an already complete object. Like the interpreting subject, the interpreted object realizes *itself* through the activity of interpretation. Because
"the sense of a text in general reaches far beyond what its author originally
intended" (Gadamer:335), the work of art harbors potentiality that *necessarily* remains unrealized by the artist. The work is finished and refinished
through the activity of responsive interpreters. Interpretation, therefore,
belongs to the very being of the object itself. Apprehension of the art object
is not a simple repetition of primordial production, but requires genuinely
creative labor in which the interpreter is aroused "to a feeling of his own
originality." "The emergent work of art," Hart observes, "depends upon
aesthetic experience that '. . . is a creative act of the same order as the act of
artistic creation.'"/29/ Expressed in Hegelian terms, the work of art is the
"work of each and all." Artistic creativity is a common cause—a joint enterprise, a corporate activity. By means of common labor, active subjects
produce the works through which they themselves assume determinate
identity. Work, regarded as activity (verb) and artifact (noun), is a complex
social process.

The sociality of the work of art discloses the productivity of distanciation.
"Interpretation, philosophically understood," Ricoeur stresses, "is nothing else
than an attempt to make estrangement and distanciation productive"
(1976:44). Artistic expression, as we have seen, is a self-objectification that
inevitably entails self-alienation. The created object assumes an independence
which eventually establishes the dependence of the creative subject. Since
l'objet d'art transcends its original producer and is completed through the
activity of others, the work returns to the artist and recreates its creator. Artist,
work, and interpreter are dialectically bound in such a way that each
continually emerges in relation to the other./30/ Creation is ever unfinished.
The Word of the Author is a call to others to join in an activity through which
their being, as well as His own, is enlarged.

V. Postcritical Faith

The interpretation of interpretation is a meta-inquiry, a transcendental
investigation which involves the effort to ascertain the conditions of the
possibility of the very act within which the subject is engaged. In the years
since the Enlightenment, literary and biblical critics have developed increasingly sophisticated methods of interpretation. When these methods are
applied to the sacred texts of a culture, the result frequently is disillusionment.

For some this development is regarded as an invaluable gain, for others an irreparable loss, for all an undeniably significant chapter in the emergence of human self-consciousness. The critical temper of modernity brings with it a loss of immediate belief or primitive naiveté. Paradoxically, however, the hand that inflicts this wound and brings malaise also bears a remedy. For those who become disillusioned with disillusionment, interpretation offers a possibility to hear again. The "second immediacy that we seek and the second naiveté that we await," Ricoeur suggests, "are no longer accessible to us anywhere else than in a hermeneutics; we can believe only by interpreting. It is the 'modern' mode of belief in symbols, an expression of the distress of modernity and a remedy for that distress" (1969:351, 352). By comprehending the alien and by recovering the familiar which has become strange, we can begin to overcome the estrangement so often engendered by criticism. It is clear, however, that postcritical faith is impossible apart from interpretation. But no longer can we afford to stop here. Responsible agency always presupposes self-consciousness. Interpretation, therefore, is not enough. We must move from reflection to reflexion, from criticism to metacriticism by interpreting interpretation. Only when we understand understanding do we realize that "the final belief is to believe in a fiction, which you know to be a fiction, there being nothing else. The exquisite truth is to know that it is a fiction and that you believe it willingly" (Stevens:163).

Notes

/1/   Previous theories of interpretation were, by contrast, regional. Instead of trying to identify general rules of interpretation which would be applicable to any text, analysts focused attention on a particular field of inquiry such as classical, juridical, or theological studies.

/2/   Throughout this paper, I am primarily concerned with the problem of the written text. This point should be kept in mind as we proceed to the analysis of the work of art. For a consideration of the hermeneutical problems peculiar to writing, see, *inter alia*: Ricoeur, "Speaking and Writing," 1976:25–44, and Jacques Derrida, *Writing and Difference* (Chicago: University of Chicago Press, 1978).

/3/   This line of analysis recently has been revived by E. D. Hirsch in *Validity in Interpretation* (New Haven: Yale University Press, 1967).

/4/   In this context, "hermeneutics" does not refer to the general theory of interpretation, but designates a particular movement of thought which grows out of Heidegger's philosophy. Though Heidegger's impact on this area of inquiry has been considerable, we shall focus on the work of Gadamer as representative of this tradition.

/5/   Culler clarifies this point when he notes that "'subject' in this context means the subject of experience, the 'I' or self which thinks, perceives, speaks, and so on" (80).

/6/ Barthes's awareness of the theological implications of his position is apparent in the following text: "In precisely this way literature . . . , by refusing to assign a 'secret,' an ultimate meaning, to the text (and to the world as text), liberates what may be called an anti-theological activity, an activity that is truly revolutionary since to refuse to fix meaning is, in the end, to refuse God" (1977:147).

It should be noted that in his later work Barthes moves beyond structuralism and expresses deep-going criticism of many central tenets of structuralist methodology.

/7/   See Ricoeur, "Structure and Hermeneutics" (1974:27–61).

/8/   These are Ricoeur's terms (1970:459ff.).

/9/   This point, of course, is borrowed from Hegel. As we shall see in the next section, the effort to resolve the *aporiai* created by the Cartesian analysis of the subject and the object forms the foundation of the *Phenomenology of Spirit*.

/10/   We shall return to this central issue in section four. At that time the basis of Gadamer's claim will become clearer. For a different statement of this point of view, see Wolfgang Iser, *The Act of Reading: A Theory of Aesthetic Response* (Baltimore: Johns Hopkins University Press, 1978).

/11/   It is obvious that the strictures of this essay force us to condense our remarks and to pass over the subtle, but important, differences *within* each tradition. For more detailed studies, see: Richard E. Palmer, *Hermeneutics: Interpretation Theory in Schleiermacher, Dilthey, Heidegger, and Gadamer* (Evanston: Northwestern University Press, 1969); Richard R. Niebuhr, *Schleiermacher on Christ and Religion* (New York: Charles Scribner's Sons, 1964); Robert R. Williams, *Schleiermacher the Theologian: The Construction of the Doctrine of God* (Philadelphia: Fortress Press, 1978); Robert Scholes, Jonathan Culler, and Howard Gardner, *The Quest for Mind* (New York: Knopf, 1973); and Robert Funk, *Language, Hermeneutic, and Word of God* (New York: Harper & Row, 1966).

/12/   This classification of Gadamer might seem questionable. The constant emphasis on tradition appears to be at odds with the suggestion that Gadamer's hermeneutics is concerned chiefly with the future. The profound influence which Heidegger exercised on Gadamer, however, leads to a view of historicity in which the future assumes priority. Tradition, therefore, is significant more for the future it projects than for the past it recollects.

/13/   I consider these matters in greater detail in *Journeys to Selfhood: Hegel and Kierkegaard* (Berkeley: University of California Press). See especially chapter 6.

/14/   Where necessary, I have corrected the English translation. In each case the reference to Hoffmeister's German edition follows the citation of Miller's edition of the *Phenomenology*.

/15/   This way of making the point underscores the distinction between the perspectives of observing and observed consciousness. What the phenomenological observer sees in the struggle for recognition becomes evident to experiencing consciousness only at the stage of practical reason.

/16/   In this and similar passages, Hegel presents a striking anticipation of the Freudian notion of sublimation.

/17/   See Josiah Royce, *Lectures in Modern Idealism* (New Haven: Yale University Press, 1964), pp. 136ff. The word *action* might also be used for *Sache*. Such a translation further distinguishes *Sache* from *Ding*, the term Hegel uses in his analysis of theoretical reason.

/18/   The word *allgemein* can be translated "universal" or "common."

/19/   Hegel's account of *die Sache selbst* reveals the implications of the intersubjectivity of spirit which were anticipated by the phenomenological observer in reflection upon consciousness' struggle for recognition. Since the common cause explicitly exhibits the structure of spirit, the consideration of practical reason forms the transition to the long section entitled "Der Geist."

/20/   "The Fall of Hyperion: A Dream," Canto I, 11. 8–15, *The Norton Anthology of English Literature*, ed. M. H. Abrams, et al. (New York: Norton and Norton, 1979), p. 851.

/21/   As our argument unfolds, it is important to recall that we are chiefly concerned with written works of art.

/22/   It should be evident that this position implies a broad notion of the unconscious. In addition to deciphering psychological forces, it is important to listen to social and cultural notes sounding through the author's voice. Above all it is necessary to recognize the way in which "language performs thought" (Gadamer:491ff.). Not only universal linguistic codes, but also historically transmitted meanings speak through the speaker. Though it is true, as Ricoeur stresses, that "languages do not speak, people do" (1976:13), it is equally true, as structuralists contend, that without *langue* there can be no *parole*.

/23/   The converse, of course, is also true. To understand the world is, at least in part, to understand its artistic objectification. Here lies further evidence of the ever present hermeneutical circle.

/24/   Mackey makes this point in the context of analyzing Kierkegaard's view of poetry and the poet. Kierkegaard's notion of indirect communication anticipates many of the insights of contemporary hermeneutical theories developed by Gadamer and Ricoeur. Previous remarks make clear my disagreement with Mackey's dismissal of the expressive character of utterance.

/25/   See, *inter alia*, "The Effectiveness of Symbols" (1967:186–205).

/26/   In this case, the author's work is viewed as expressing universal cognitive and linguistic structures, rather than merely individual intention. Given the orientation of this study, it is interesting to note the similarity between Hegel and the structuralists on the issue of the relation between individuality and universality.

/27/   Certain metaphors are suggestive in this regard. We often speak of "consuming a work," "devouring a book," and, more colloquially, we say that an audience which is appreciative of a performance "eats it up." In this context it is well to recall Feuerbach's observation: "We are what we eat."

/28/   The relation of interpreter and text is dialectical in the original sense of the term. Interpretation establishes a dialogue between the text and the interpreter in which each questions and answers the other. The activity of the interpreter should not obscure the correlative activity of the text.

/29/   Hart's quotation is from Milton C. Nahm, *Genius and Creativity* (New York: Harper Torchbooks, 1965), p. 248.

/30/   As Gadamer maintains, "the discovery of the true meaning of a text or a work of art is never finished; it is in fact an infinite process" (265). The recognition of the processive character of the work of art and the act of interpretation underscores the insufficiency of any hermeneutics which concentrates on synchronic aspects of the text at the expense of diachronic factors. Since the text is a *continuous* emergent, a satisfactory theory of interpretation must acknowledge not only the temporality of the subject, but also the historicity of the object. It should be evident that this line of argument is not intended to deny the significance of structural analysis. Rather, the point to be emphasized is that both synchronicity and diachronicity must be taken seriously. In this section of the essay, we have attempted to establish the possibility of integrating insights of romanticists, structuralists, and hermeneuticists by reconsidering the relation of artist, work, and interpreter.

Works Consulted

Barthes, Roland
    1975   *The Pleasure of the Text*. Trans. R. Miller. New York: Hill and Wang.
    1977   *Image, Music, Text*. Trans. S. Heath. New York: Hill and Wang.

Culler, Jonathan
    1973   *Structuralist Poetics*. London: Routledge and Kegan Paul.

Gadamer, Hans-Georg
    1975   *Truth and Method*. New York: Seabury Press.

Hart, Ray L.
    1968   *Unfinished Man and the Imagination*. New York: Herder and Herder.

Hegel, G. W. F.
    1977   *Phenomenology of Spirit*. Trans. A. V. Miller. New York: Oxford University Press.

Heidegger, Martin
  1962   *Being and Time.* Trans. J. Macquarrie and E. Robinson. New
          York: Harper & Row.
  1971   *Poetry, Language, Thought.* Trans. A. Hofstadter. New York:
          Harper & Row.

Hyppolite, Jean
  1974   *Genesis and Structure of Hegel's Phenomenology of Spirit.*
          Trans. S. Cherniak and J. Heckman. Evanston: Northwestern
          University Press.

Lévi-Strauss, Claude
  1967   *Structural Anthropology.* Trans. C. Jacobson. New York:
          Doubleday.

Mackey, Louis
  1972   *Kierkegaard: A Kind of Poet.* Philadelphia: University of
          Pennsylvania Press.

Ricoeur, Paul
  1969   *The Symbolism of Evil.* Trans. E. Buchanan. Boston: Beacon
          Press.
  1970   *Freud and Philosophy: An Essay on Interpretation.* Trans.
          D. Savage. New Haven: Yale University Press.
  1974   *The Conflict of Interpretations: Essays in Hermeneutics.* Ed.
          D. Idhe. Evanston: Northwestern University Press.
  1976   *Interpretation Theory: Discourse and the Surplus of Mean-*
          ing. Fort Worth: Texas Christian University Press.

Schleiermacher, Friedrich
  1978   *Hermeneutics: The Handwritten Manuscripts.* Trans. J. Forst-
          man and J. Duke. Missoula, MT: Scholars Press.

Scholes, Robert
  1974   *Structuralism in Literature.* New Haven: Yale University
          Press.

Stevens, Wallace
  1957   *Opus Posthumous,* Ed. S. F. Morse. New York: Alfred A.
          Knopf.

The Empty Mirror

The proficiency of our finest scholars, their heedless industry, their heads
smoking day and night, their very craftsmanship—how often the real
meaning of all this lies in the desire to keep something hidden from oneself!
Science as a means of self-narcosis: *do you have experience of that?*

Nietzsche

I. Reflections

In his seminal work, *The Metamorphosis of the Gods*, André Malraux
describes a series of Van Eyck's paintings which culminates in the well-
known "The Goldsmith Jan de Leeuw" (1436): "These pictures were not
made for churches. Nor for Bibles, like the Carolingian portraits . . . ; nor
even for Books of Hours. Though stemming from religious imagery, they
no longer derived their value from the service of God. Nor from what they
represented, for their subjects interested only a few people; nor from their
illusionism alone. Actually *trompe-l'oeil* effects play no greater part in *Jean
de Leeuw* than they do in *Mona Lisa*. Yet, even assuming that the former
was relatively little like its model, it would still suggest to contemporaries
an attempt to vie with the forms of the created world—and this even
without Van Eyck's skillful shading, since portraits by the Flemalle Master
and Van der Wyeden reveal a similar attempt. Donors had always been
shown gazing towards Christ or the Madonna, but the eyes of Jean de
Leeuw . . . are turned *toward the painter*" (368). The significance of the
seemingly innocent shift of the Goldsmith's eyes becomes apparent when
this painting is placed within the context of an overall artistic development
which Malraux charts. The history of art, according to Malraux, displays a
gradual desacralization or secularization in which the function of art shifts
from the representation of the gods to the expression of an autonomous
realm ruled by the artist which Cézanne eventually labeled *la peinture*.
While it is neither possible nor necessary to rehearse Malraux's complex
argument, a brief comparison of his interpretation of Byzantine art as
illustrated by the Ravenna mosaics and Van Eyck's "The Madonna of
Chancellor Rolin" suggests the general direction of his analysis and sets the
stage for our exploration of the post-modern death of selfhood.

Like its most successful architectural achievement, Hagia Sophia, Byzantine mosaics are, for Malraux, essentially hieratic. Reflecting major tendencies

in much eastern orthodox theology, Byzantine art focuses on the eternal Christ to the virtual exclusion of the historical Jesus. As is evident in the Ravenna "Parable of the Last Judgment," the heavenly Christ is characteristically surrounded by an ethereal, otherworldly ambiance. The use of color and lack of perspective serve a common purpose: "a *disincarnation* as deliberate and far more drastic than the idealizations of an earlier art—a means of giving human beings access to the world of Truth" (143). Allusion to the transcendent sacred, rather than illusion of mundane reality, was the aim of Byzantine artistic endeavor.

When Van Eyck's "The Madonna of Chancellor Rolin" is placed alongside the Ravenna mosaic, the contrast is striking. Gone is the timeless Christ and in his place we find a radically new object of devotion—a babe on the knee of his mother. Van Eyck domesticates the sacred by placing the encounter with the divine within the *home* of the patron. The "unreal" colors and one dimensionality of the mosaic give way to the realistic light, shadow, and depth of the painting. The world of appearance no longer points beyond itself to a transcendent realm of Truth, but has become the domain in which the divine is incarnate. And it is toward this timely appearance of God that the Chancellor directs his gaze.

But the Goldsmith, as we have seen, shifts his eyes—away from the disincarnate sacred, away from the incarnate divine, toward the painter. "Once the Crucifixion entered into Time," Malraux points out, "portraits won their entry into painting" (367). Emancipated from the divine, the Goldsmith no longer derives justification from implicit or explicit association with the sacred. Jan de Leeuw's eyes reflect a new recognition of the power vested in the *artist*. The position once held by the Creator now is assumed by the creative artist.

The final step in the progression we are following emerges when we turn our attention to a painting which Malraux does not mention, Velazquez's "The Maids of Honor" (1656). Michel Foucault, of course, begins his brilliant *Les Mots et Les Choses* with a detailed analysis of this painting. For our purposes, three features of Velazquez's work merit attention: the painter, the Infanta, and the mirror. "The Maids of Honor" represents an interesting inversion of Van Eyck's "Goldsmith." Rather than the subject gazing at the artist, the artist is shown looking at the subject. Foucault notes how "The painter is looking, his face is turned slightly and his head leaning towards one shoulder. He is staring at a point to which, even though it is invisible, we, the spectators, can easily assign an object, since it is we, ourselves, who are that point: our bodies, our faces, our eyes" (1970:4). This outward thrust is emphasized by the picture's principal figure. At the center of the painting we discover not the infant Jesus, but a child princess, attended by a maid of honor whose kneeling posture recalls an adoring donor similar to Chancellor Rolin. However, unlike the Christ child, the princess arrests our gaze only to turn our attention *away* from herself, for she too is looking outward, toward the spectator. The point of convergence of the stares of artist and princess is suggested by the mirror which stands above the child's head. In this somewhat obscure looking-glass, we can discern the images of King Philip IV and his wife, Mariana. The more we reflect on this reflection, however, the more puzzling it becomes. The mirror, it seems, conceals as much as it reveals. "That space where the king and his wife hold sway belongs equally well to the artist and to the spectator; in the depths of the mirror there could also appear—there ought to appear—the anonymous face of the passer-by and that of Velazquez." Not only the artist, but we ourselves seem to have disappeared in a play of mirrors. Foucault concludes that "in the midst of this dispersion which it [i.e., the painting] is simultaneously grouping together and spreading out before us, indicated compellingly from every side, is an essential void: the necessary disappearance of that which is its foundation—of the person it resembles and the person in whose eyes it is only a resemblance. This very subject—which is the same—has been elided" (1970:16). Sartre's Estelle might well have been looking at "The Maids of Honor" when she reflects, "I feel so queer. . . . When I can't see myself, I begin to wonder if I really and truly exist. I pat myself just to make sure, but it doesn't help much. . . . I've six big mirrors in my bedroom. They are there. I can see them. But they don't see me . . . how empty it is, a glass in which I'm absent!" (1955:20) Velazquez's painting makes visible our invisibility by presenting our absence. First the transcendent God, then the incarnate Christ, and finally the self itself disappear—die.

II. The Disappearance of Author-ity

It is commonly acknowledged that a fundamental feature of modernism is the death of God. Less often recognized is that one of the chief characteristics of post-modernism is the death of selfhood. In what follows, I shall argue that these two dimensions of contemporary experience are closely related: the death of God finds its completion in the death of selfhood. This line of argument rejects the common belief that the death of God entails the liberation and actualization of the individual self. I shall conclude by suggesting that *if* theology is to have a future, we must learn to speak of God godlessly and of self selflessly.

Central to the modern eclipse of God is the critique of authority which developed during the latter part of the eighteenth century. Although rooted in Reformation theology and descendent from spiritualistic heirs of the radical reformers, the heart of the Enlightenment critique of authority was the renewed confidence in human reason. "*Sapere aude!*" declared Kant. "Have courage to use your own reason!—that is the motto of enlightenment" (3). As Kant's own position makes clear, critique did not necessarily mean rejection. To the contrary, authority was maintained, though internalized; heteronomy was translated into autonomy as the word of one became the voice of all. The apparent universality of reason seemed to provide a safeguard against relativistic historicism and to preclude the solipsism implicit in egalitarianism. While Kant believed his elaborate philosophical enterprise to be in the service of faith, the recognition of the inextricable relation between Author and authority led more radical thinkers of the era to less positive conclusions about religious belief and practice. Since human emancipation and religious liberation often were deemed inseparable, many argued that the chains of authority could be broken only by the death of the founding father. It is not too much to say that revolution became secular communion. The fraternal bond joining the sons of the Revolution was forged by common participation in the act of partricide and was sealed by the blood of the slain Father.

Though at odds with Kant's own perspective, the radicalism of post-Kantian thought was an understandable outgrowth of his critical philosophy. The Romantic veneration of creative individuality and preoccupation with historical process cast doubt upon the purported universality of Kant's forms of intuition and categories of understanding. Throughout the nineteenth century, increasing sensitivity to the historicity of consciousness led to decreasing belief in agenetic epistemic structures. This development had important consequences for the interpretation of religious belief. Having recognized the social, cultural, and psychological conditions of consciousness, thinkers as diverse as Hegel, Marx, Nietzsche, and Freud examined religious thought and conduct in an effort to discern the latent content of manifest awareness. Though the analyses of these "hermeneuticists of suspicion" differed widely, all agreed that what had for centuries been regarded as objective reality was, in fact, nothing more than a subjective projection. Inverting the traditional Creator/creature relation, God was regarded merely as an expression of human desire, misery, or will to power.

As a result of these social, political, and intellectual upheavals, "the authority of a privileged Origin that commands, guarantees, and perpetuates meaning [was] removed" (Said:315). The death of God was the disappearance of the Author who had inscribed absolute truth and univocal meaning in world history and human experience. As in one of Robbe-Grillet's plotless novels, the narrative thread unraveled leaving a text to be interpreted in place of a story to be uncovered. The death of God created an "interpretive imperative." Since the world text no longer had an authoritative author who established its intrinsic intelligibility, interpretation by necessity became creative rather than imitative. *Poiesis*, in other words, replaced *mimesis*. The range of such creative interpretation appeared to be limitless. As Derrida points out, "The absence of a transcendental signified stretches the field and the play of significations to infinity" (1978:289). Nietzsche, the first person to recognize the profound hermeneutical implications of the death of God, put the point succinctly and provocatively: "There are no facts, only interpretations."

The reaction to the disappearance of Author-ity extended from defensive rejection or anxious acknowledgment to enthusiastic acceptance. Two typical responses which are especially important for our purposes might be labeled Hegelian unhappy consciousness and Nietzschean joyous affirmation. Let us consider each of these in turn.

Echoing Roquetin's lament that "the world stays on my lips: it refuses to go and put itself on the thing" (1964:125), Foucault correctly contends that "the threshold between Classicism and modernity . . . had been definitively crossed when words ceased to intersect with representations and to provide a spontaneous grid for the knowledge of things" (1970:304). Within the domain of literature, as J. Hillis Miller suggests, modernity is characterized by the break between symbol and symbolized in which there is an increasing loss of participation. The poetry of presence gives way to the poetry of absence in which language is self-referential, or in Jakobson's term, "autotelic." Language, in other words, is not rooted in and does not point toward an extra-linguistic referent. Though this point of view was given its most influential formulation in Saussure's linguistic theory, the discerning eye can recognize its lineaments in major eighteenth- and nineteenth-century figures./1/ The price which Kant paid for the intelligibility of human reason was the unintelligibility of the world in itself. With the disappearance or unknowability of the transcendent Origin of order, the intrinsic meaning of nature and history was eclipsed./2/ As we have seen, order, if present at all, had to be made and could not be discovered. Roland Barthes might well be describing Kant when he stresses that we never have immediate access to the pure world, but must "encode" it to experience it. When the rise of historicism called into question the universality of our cognitive categories, it became apparent that the relation between subject and object, or sign and referent, to say nothing of the relation between signifier and signified, is arbitrary. Semantic forms that Kant and many others had regarded as a priori now appear to be a posteriori, that is, conventions of particular linguistic communities. We might summarize this conclusion by suggesting that the death of God paves the way for the birth of the sign, the sign whose distinctive traits are its conventionality and its external relation to and thus arbitrary association with the signified, be it real or ideal. "In the work of an artist like Hölderlin," Edward Said points out, we find "commemorated simultaneously the death of God and the new sovereign status of language, the connected problematics of absence and presence, and beneath those, the complex interplay of signifiers detached from a stable signified that results . . . from the 'no' filling the (dead) father's place: all this is made possible when the world is no longer conceived as representation, but instead, Foucault says . . . as *interpretation*" (305). The death of God, the disappearance of the Father, is the birth of the Son, the appearance of the Word—the appearance of language as sovereign.

"*La libération du significant*,"/3/ however, harbors darkness. Truth a fiction, certainty a dream, the world becomes an unfathomable abyss and human experience utterly abysmal. With the disappearance of the Primal Origin, the meaning of experience becomes obscure and a sense of transcendental homelessness develops. Like Hegel's unhappy consciousness, selves become exiles who wander through a labyrinthian world nostalgically recollecting and hopefully anticipating, but never arriving. "Nausea," Dominic Crossan points out, is "the ontological disappointment of one who, having been taught that there is some overarching logical meaning beyond our perception, has come at length to believe there is no such fixed center towards which our searchings strive" (72). When homeless sojourners speak, they seem imprisoned in an echo chamber and, like one of Joyce's characters, hear only themselves. But when they look, the mirror is empty.

Summarizing what we have defined as unhappy consciousness, Derrida describes a contrasting response to the disappearance of Author-ity: "Turned towards the lost or impossible presence of the absent origin, this structuralist thematic of broken immediacy is therefore the saddened, *negative*, nostalgic, guilty, Rousseauistic side of the thinking of play whose other side would be the Nietzschean *affirmation*, that is the joyous affirmation of the play of the world and of the innocence of becoming, the affirmation of a world of signs without fault, without truth, and without origin which is offered to an active interpretation. *This affirmation then determines the noncenter otherwise than as loss of the center*. And it plays without security. For there is a *sure* play: that which is limited to the *substitution* of *given* and *existing, present*, pieces. In absolute chance, affirmation also surrenders itself to *genetic* indetermination, to the *seminal* adventure of the trace" (1978:292). For Nietzsche, as for many of his recent followers, the death of the Creator liberates the power of human creativity. The self-confident Zarathustra anticipates the Derridean interpretive imperative when he proclaims, "You should learn *only* to create!" (Nietzsche, 1957:212) Los appears divine, it seems, only when Urizen is slain./4/ Released from the unhappiness of repressive univocality and monocularity, seemingly happy, joyous selves set sail on the "Sea of ex,"/5/ free to interpret playfully and to enjoy the plurivocal and polysemous products of their creation. The abiding recognition that signifiers float freely above an abyss that is at least "70,000 fathoms" deep only intensifies the fury of this "bacchanalian revel."

Protests to the contrary notwithstanding, there seems to be something anxious and frantic in this frenzy. Zarathustra's herculean self-assurance appears curiously fragile. Careful reflection discloses striking similarities between Nietzsche's joyous affirmation and Hegel's comic awareness. Hegel describes comedy when he writes:

> What this self-consciousness beholds is that whatever assumes the form of essentiality over against it, is instead dissolved in it—in its thinking, its

existence, and its action—and is at its mercy. It is the return of everything
universal into the certainty of itself which, in consequence, is this complete
loss of fear and of essential being on the part of all that is alien. This self-
certainty is a state of spiritual being and of repose such as is not be to found
anywhere outside of this comedy. (1977:452–53)

In Hegel's dialectical vision, however, opposites are implicitly identical. The
ostensibly happy consciousness of the comic subject is, in fact, unhappy.
"Unhappy consciousness," he argues, "constitutes the reverse side of the
fulfillment of comic consciousness that is perfectly happy within itself. Into
this consciousness, all divine being returns, or it is the complete *alienation* of
substance. Unhappy consciousness, on the other hand, is, conversely, the
tragic fate of the certainty of self that aims to be absolute. It is the
consciousness of the loss of all essential being in this *certainty of itself*, and
of the loss even of this knowledge about itself—the loss of substance as well
as of the self, it is the grief which expresses itself in the hard saying that
'God is dead'" (1977:454–55). The death of God and the loss of self. Even in
Nietzsche's joyous affirmation, perhaps decisively in this affirmation, we
again discover the empty mirror.

III. The Disappearance of Selfhood

Commenting on the coimplication of Blake's satanic "Nobodaddy"
named Urizen and "slumberous" solitary selfhood, Thomas Altizer writes:
"Good and evil cease to be when man is delivered from Self-hood, when his
solitary and autonomous ego is abolished, and he ceases to be aware of a
distance separating himself from others. That very distance is solidified by
the demands of a distant Lord, and apart from a fallen confinement in an
isolated selfhood there could be no awareness of God as the Wholly Other"
(1967:200). Heralded in Blake's apocalyptic poetry and anticipated in
Kierkegaard's ironic prose, the death of selfhood, which has been realized
concretely in twentieth-century sociopolitical and technological developments, has only recently found forceful expression. We can hear this anonymous voice clearly in two seminal contemporary movements of thought:
structuralism and post-structuralist deconstruction. Structuralism and deconstruction assault the self from opposite directions—the former detemporal-
izes and the latter radically temporalizes the subject. Selfhood disintegrates
either in systematic synchronicity or in fragmented diachronicity.

Said's apt summary of conclusions reached by several major French
thinkers suggests the far-reaching implications of structural analysis: "Man is
dissolved in the overarching waves, in the quanta, the striations of language
itself, turning finally into little more than a constituted subject, a speaking
pronoun, fixed indecisively in the eternal, ongoing rush of discourse" (287).
Departing decisively from most post-Cartesian philosophy, structuralism
decenters the subject by shifting the locus of intentionality from the *cogito*

to conventional interpersonal systems which operate through the ego. Lévi-Strauss goes so far as to argue that "the goal of the human sciences is not to constitute man, but to dissolve him" (326). This point of view is not narrowly partisan, but emerges from the convergence of insights garnered from multiple perspectives. According to Foucault, "The researches of psychoanalysis, of linguistics, of anthropology, have 'decentered' the subject in relation to the laws of its desire, the forms of its language, the rules of its actions, or the play of its mythical and imaginative discourse" (1969:22). While these contrasting angles of vision highlight different aspects of the anthropological problematic, there is a general agreement that concrete individuality can be understood only in terms of systematic totality. Be it with Heidegger's *Sprache*, Saussure's *langue*, Greimas's *modèl actantiel*, Chomsky's generative grammar, Propp's plot, Jakobson's poetic function, Lacan's unconscious, Barthes's codes, or Foucault's *episteme*, temporal particularity is resolved into atemporal generality or universality. Heidegger's formula provides a structure in which terms can be substituted to provide various expressions of this common insight. "Language speaks [Die Sprache *spricht*]. Man speaks only insofar as he artfully complies with language" (161).

What, then, is the individual self which for so many appears to be the foundation of reality? Foucault insists that the individual subject as the ground of a philosophical anthropology is "a recent invention" within human knowledge which is rendered possible by a peculiar configuration of human experience. With the passing of the *episteme* whose invention man is, man will be "erased, like a face drawn in sand at the edge of the sea" (1970:386–87) or we might add like a face that refuses to appear in the artist's empty mirror. Rather than a concrete actuality, the individual self is a "paper I" (Barthes:79), a fictive construction which is really nothing other than a "discursive function." With the dissolution of the purposeful individual in the post-modern world, the enunciative subject is no longer the primal origin of discourse and it thus loses its position of "judge, teacher, analyst, confessor, or decoder" (Barthes:81). This disappearance of the subject is, according to Barthes, "the death of the author." The erasure of the author is the closure of authorized meaning which opens the *"social* space" of the text to the pleasurable play of interpretation./6/ Although not generally noted, the death of the author consummates the death of the Author. The effort to preserve the integral self, like the struggle to cling to God, represents a nostalgic longing for truth and certainty which long since have grown tenuous. To the tutored eye, the close relation of the death of God and of self is apparent in Foucault's contention that "the author does not precede the works, he is a certain functional principle by which, in our culture, one limits, excludes, and chooses, in short, by which one impedes the free circulation, the free manipulation, the free composition, decomposition, and recomposition of fiction. . . . One can say that the author is an ideological product, since we represent him as the opposite of his historically real function. . . . The author is therefore the ideological figure by which one marks the manner in which we fear the proliferation of meaning" (1979:159). Said captures the latent mood of this erasure of the self when he writes: "The structuralists share a gloomy theme in the idea of loss and, associated with it, man's unhappy historical insertion into a language game that he can barely understand" (315).

The extent to which this unhappy consciousness overshadows the present landscape becomes apparent in the post-structuralists' deconstruction of the constructed subject. As we have pointed out, in opposition to structuralism, deconstruction dissolves the self by radically temporalizing the subject. Derrida, the most important proponent of deconstruction, maintains that despite protests to the contrary, structuralism remains essentially conservative and perpetuates what he calls the "metaphysics of presence" which has dominated Western reflection. Synchronic structures which are supposed to constitute the individual self are the latest manifestation of the atemporal forms which, since Plato, have been imagined to mitigate the distress of our ineradicable temporality. With Heidegger's account of the inseparability of being and time, however, a frame of reference emerges which marks the closure of the metaphysics of presence. When we think time radically, the original self or the perduring subject disappears and in its place we find only an elusive trace—a mark of a presence that is always absent or a sign of an absence that is never present.

The basis of Derrida's critique of presence is most accessible in his early book, *Speech and Phenomena*. The argument is predictable. Derrida attempts to demonstrate that Husserl's phenomenology is but a variation of the metaphysics of presence. What is most interesting is Derrida's contention, in good deconstructionist fashion, that at the heart of Husserl's analysis of internal time consciousness lie tendencies which, if developed, would lead to the self-negation of this phenomenology. These seeds come to fruition in the work of Husserl's pupil, Heidegger, and in Heidegger's pupil, Derrida.

Derrida maintains that the metaphysics of presence is bound up with an understanding of time in which the essential ecstasy is the "punctual present." This primal moment is the condition of the possibility of the *self*-consciousness which marks the beginning and the end of the Western philosophical tradition. The presence of the self to itself in self-consciousness is inseparable from the present's presence of itself to itself in the now. The present, in other words, is the "source point" from which the self originates. But as Hegel had recognized/7/ and as Husserl suggests, the *hic et nunc* is fugitive—disappearing in the very act of appearing. Heidegger's "temporalizing temporalization" in which "the transcendental horizon of the question of being" is "freed from the traditional and metaphysical domination by the present or the now," lays the foundation for Derrida's contention that the "living present" "is always already a trace" (1973:139–

85). As the re-presentation of a former presence, the present is an absence, a trace of a presence that never is present.

With the displacement of the present, the self disappears. "The self of the living present," Derrida insists, "is primordially a trace" (1973:85)./8/ To the extent that the self is believed to be "real," creative fiction is mistaken for an established fact. Literal consciousness repeats its theological projection of a transcendent Author by first imagining and then reifying the authorizing presence of selfhood. Literal consciousness, therefore, has no recognition that the self is, in Barthes's fine phràse, "a metaphor without brakes." Explaining Nietzsche's deliteralization of the language of the self, from which so much of Derrida's deconstruction of subjectivity derives, Paul de Man explains that "faced with the truth of its non-existence, the self would be consumed by the flame that attracts it. But the text that asserts this annihilation of the self is not consumed, because it still sees itself as the center that produces the affirmation. The attributes of centrality and of selfhood are being exchanged in the medium of language. Making the language that denies the self into a center rescues the self linguistically at the same point that it asserts its insignificance, its emptiness as a mere figure of speech. It can only persist as self if it is displaced into the text that denies it. The self which was at first the center of the language as its empirical referent now becomes the language of the center as fiction, as metaphor of the self. What was originally simply a referential text now becomes the text of a text, the figure of a figure. The deconstruction of the self as a metaphor does not end in the rigorous separation of the two categories (self and figure) from each other but ends instead in an exchange of properties that allows for their mutual persistence at the expense of literal truth" (40).

The transmutation of the problem of selfhood into the problem of textuality points to a final correlation between the death of God and the death of selfhood. As we have seen, the death of God was the disappearance of the Author who had inscribed absolute truth and univocal meaning in world history and human experience. This led to an interpretive imperative in which creative interpretation replaced mimetic representation. The disappearance of the subject entails similar implications. As the death of God implies the birth of the Word, so the death of selfhood implies the birth of the text. The loss of the author, through either dissipation in atemporal systems or fragmentation in temporal flux, elides authoritative meaning and decenters the text. When "things fall apart," when "the center cannot hold," the text explodes. "The text," Barthes stresses, "is plural. This does not mean just that it has several meanings, but rather that it achieves plurality of meaning, an *irreducible* plurality. The Text is not coexistence of meanings but passage, traversal; thus it answers . . . to an explosion, a dissemination. The Text's plurality does not depend on the ambiguity of its contents, but rather on what could be called the *stereographic plurality* of the signifiers that weave it . . ." (Barthes:76). No longer in bondage to its author-father, the text is freed for permanent metamorphosis, its meaning open to ceaseless flux. The ongoing productivity of the text is realized through the act of interpretation. Such creative interpretation is possible only after Author and author have died. The disappearance of all forms of authority means that univocal meaning and certain truth are inaccessible or, as Derrida puts it, are "infinitely deferred." This deferral does not, for Derrida, engender Sartrean nausea. To the contrary, Derrida espouses the Nietzschean affirmation which, as we have noted, "is the joyous affirmation of the play of the world and of the innocence of becoming, the affirmation of a world of signs without fault, without truth, and without origin which is offered to an active interpretation. *This affirmation then determines the noncenter otherwise than as loss of the center.* And it plays without security" (1978:76).

Like comic awareness, which we have seen to be the inverse of the death of God, this joyful wisdom seems to be yet another form of unhappy consciousness. The general term which Derrida uses to describe the infinite deferral of presence is "*écriture.*" Derrida's corpus to date is, in fact, an extended grammatology in which he repeatedly underscores the absence of presence in temporal experience. It is not too much to say that Derrida attempts to replace the metaphysics of presence with a philosophy of absence and in so doing errs in the opposite direction. "Writing," Derrida insinuates, "is the moment of the desert as the moment of Separation" (1978:68). The theological implications of this cryptic remark begin to emerge when we realize that "writing and Judaism are the same waiting" (1978:68). We might join Derrida's analysis of writing and Judaism by suggesting that the consciousness of the people of the Book is *Scriptural.* "The Judaic experience as reflection, as separation of life and thought, signifies the crossing of the book as an *infinite* anchoritism placed between two immediacies and two self-identifications" (1978:68). Though the sons of Abraham have fallen from the Garden, the Messiah has yet to appear—his arrival is delayed, his presence infinitely deferred. Exiles are condemned to wander the desert nostalgically recollecting and hopefully anticipating, but never arriving. Our analysis comes full circle when we realize that for Hegel, the figure Derrida dubs the "first philosopher of writing," Jewish consciousness is quintessentially unhappy consciousness. Interestingly enough, Derrida concurs with Hegel. "The Jewish consciousness," he admits, "is indeed the unhappy consciousness . . ." (1978:68). In a manner not unlike Derrida's own practice of deconstruction, Hegel identifies in unhappy consciousness the inherent opposite which leads to its self-negation. For Hegel, the death of selfhood is part of

> the painful feeling of the unhappy consciousness that *God Himself is dead.* This hard saying is the expression of innermost simple self-knowledge, the return of consciousness into the depths of the night in which 'I' = 'I', a night which no longer distinguishes or knows anything outside of it. This feeling is, in fact, the loss of substance and of its appearance over against consciousness;

but it is at the same time the pure *subjectivity* of substance, or the pure
certainty of itself which it lacked when it was object, or the immediate, or
pure essence. This knowing is the inspiration of spirit, whereby substance
becomes subject, by which its abstraction and lifelessness have died, and
substance therefore has become *actual* and simple and universal self-
consciousness. (1977:476)

The sublation of unhappy consciousness points the way toward the
dialectical interplay of identity-and-difference in which the problems of a
philosophy of presence are overcome without falling prey to the pitfalls of a
philosophy of absence. By so doing, Hegel creates the possibility of
reviewing and renewing both God and selfhood.

IV. Negative Dialectics

In this final section, I shall explore further theological implications of the
disappearance of Author-ity and the death of selfhood by using Hegel's
concept of negativity to examine the closely associated notions of difference
and relation. In this way I shall attempt to show that the labyrinthian chaos
we have uncovered is nothing other than the scene of redemption, the
birthplace of Hegel's universal self-consciousness which is the self-realization
of *both* God and self. After all, as Eliot suggests in "Burnt Norton," "Only
through time time is conquered."

Thomas Altizer, one of the few contemporary thinkers to have stressed
the importance of the work of Hegel for the themes we are probing, is
keenly aware of the significance of the empty mirror.

Once the ground of an autonomous consciousness has been emptied or dissolved, then there can be no individual center of consciousness, or no center
which is autonomous and unique. With the disappearance of the ground of
individual selfhood, the unique 'I' or personal ego progressively becomes a
mere reflection or echo of its former self. Now the 'I' takes into itself
everything from which it had withdrawn itself, and therefore it ceases to
stand apart. In losing its autonomy, it loses its own unique center or ground,
and thereby it loses everything which had once appeared as an individual
identity or 'face.' Facelessness and loss of identity now become the mark of
everyone, as everyone becomes no one, and the 'I' is inseparable from the
'other.' Individual selfhood does not simply or literally come to an end or
disappear; it appears in the other. Only in the other does the individual
appear or become real, for it is only in the eyes or the glance or the touch of
the other that the individual becomes himself. (1979:155)

In stressing the contrasts between the analyses of selfhood developed in
structuralism and in deconstruction, we have overlooked important similarities
they share. The synchronic emphasis of structuralism and the diachronic
preoccupation of deconstruction are joined by a common appreciation for
Saussure's insistence that difference defines identity. Saussure contends that
language is essentially a system of relations in which terms are differentially

defined. In his seminal phrase, *"dans la langue il n'y a que des différences sans termes positifs."* Saussure explains this point in more detail in his highly influential *Course in General Linguistics*. "Everything that has been said up to this point boils down to this: in language there are only differences. Even more important: a difference generally implies positive terms between which the difference is set up; but in language there are only differences *without positive terms*. Whether we take the signified or the signifier, language has neither ideas nor sounds that existed before the linguistic system, but only conceptual and phonic differences that have issued from the system" (120). The determinate identity of any particularity, in other words, is a function of relation to otherness. When adequately comprehended, interrelated terms form a systematic synchronic totality. As Lévi-Strauss points out, "One of the most important lessons of the 'phonological revolution' was its refusal to treat terms as independent entities and its concentration on relations among terms" (Culler:11). Structuralism's dissolution of the subject is actually an extrapolation of Saussure's insight into the differential character of identity, which ends by regarding man as essentially a structure of intersecting relations. "No longer a coherent *cogito*," Said writes, "man now inhabits the interstices, 'the vacant interstellar spaces,' not as an object, still less as a subject; rather, man is the *structure*, the generality of relationships among those words and ideas that we call the humanistic, as opposed to the pure, or natural, sciences" (286).

Derrida extends Saussure's semiological *différence* through his own *différance*, a notion which he believes brings together "what has been most decisively inscribed in the thought of . . . our 'epoch'" (1973:130). Derrida's *différance* supplements Saussure's *différence* by adding diachronic deferral to synchronic spacing. Drawing upon Saussure's recognition of the interplay of identity and difference, Derrida maintains that "non-presence and otherness are internal to presence" (1973:66). It is important not to confuse *différance* and difference, in the common sense of the term. *Différance*, which itself is never actually present or is present only as absence or abyss, establishes the difference which defines whatever is. In a highly suggestive statement, Derrida claims that *"différance* is the nonfull, nonsimple 'origin'; it is the structured and differing origin of differences" (1973:141). This is a remarkable formulation, for it suggests a striking similarity between Derridean *différance* and what theologians traditionally have called "God." Contrary to all expectation, Derrida offers precisely this confession.

> If the face *is body*, it is mortal. Infinite alterity as death cannot be reconciled with infinite alterity as positivity and presence (God). Metaphysical transcendence cannot be at once transcendence toward the other as Death and transcendence toward the other as God. Unless God means Death, which after all has never been *excluded* by the entirety of the classical philosophy within which we understand God both as Life and as Truth of Infinity, of positive Presence. But what does this *exclusion* mean if not the exclusion of

every particular *determination*? And that God is *nothing* (determined), is not
life, because he is *everything*? And therefore is at once All and Nothing, Life
and Death. Which means that God is or appears, *is named*, within the
difference between All and Nothing, Life and Death. Within this difference,
and at bottom as *difference* itself. (1978:115–16)

An examination of Hegel's notion of negativity will help to clarify this
unanticipated theological twist in the positions of structuralism and deconstruction. Saussurean *différence* and Derridean *différance* are variations of
Hegel's notion of negativity. As the foundation of the entire Hegelian
system, negativity is the essence of both God and self. Hegel develops his
analysis of negativity most fully in his consideration of the "Determinations
of Reflection" at the beginning of the second book of his *Logic*. Here Hegel
presents an extensive criticism of the abstract either-or of analytic understanding. In opposition to commonsense reflection, Hegel maintains that
"a consideration of everything that is shows that *in its own self* everything is
in its selfsameness different from itself and self-contradictory, and that in its
difference, in its contradictions, it is self-identical, and is in its own self this
movement of transition of one of these categories into the other, and for this
reason, that each is in its own self the opposite of itself" (1969:412). Hegel's
grasp of the interplay of identity, difference, and contradiction and his
appreciation of the internality of relationship anticipate the positions of both
Saussure and the structuralists on the one hand, and of Derrida and the
deconstructionists on the other. For Hegel, the identity of *both* identity and
difference is constituted and maintained by relation to otherness. "In the
first place," he writes, "each *is, only insofar as the other is*; it is what it is,
through the other, through its own non-being; . . . second, it is, *insofar* as
the other is not, it is what it is, through the non-being of the other"
(1969:425). In more general terms relations are not external to antecedent
identity, but are internal and essential to all particularity.

Hegel is convinced that this insight forces one to reexamine the foundation of traditional logic—the laws of identity and non-contradiction. According to those principles, everything is identical with itself. Stated
concisely: $A = A$. What usually remains unnoticed, Hegel insists, is that this
principle of identity is inherently self-contradictory. Those who attempt to
affirm such abstract identity "do not see that in this very assertion, they are
themselves saying that *identity is different*; for they are saying that identity
is different from difference . . ." (1969:413). Since Hegel argues for the
coimplication of identity and difference, he believes that determinate
identity establishes itself through the negation of otherness. The other,
however, is itself the negation of the determinate identity *it* opposes. Each
member of the relationship becomes itself through the negation of its own
negation. "Each therefore *is*, only insofar as its *non-being is*, and is in an
identical relationship with it" (1969:425). In more abstract terms, the
assertion "A is A" *necessarily* entails the claim that A is not non-A: $A = -\bar{A}$.

A is the negation of its own negation, and hence is double negation. The same analysis, of course, must be applied to non-A. Non-A becomes itself through relation to its opposite, A. But A has shown itself to be -$\bar{\text{A}}$. Thus non-A also forms itself through a process of double negation: -A = -(-$\bar{\text{A}}$).

In sum, the structure of constitutive relationality is negativity, understood as a process of double negation through which opposing relata coinhere. "If I say I am for myself," Hegel explains, "I not only am, but I negate all other in me, exclude it from me, insofar as it appears external. As the negation of other being which is negation over against me, being-for-self is the negation of negation, and thus is affirmation; and this is, as I call it, absolute negativity" (1968a:302–3). The specific example which Hegel chooses to illustrate his point suggests the close connection between his logical and theological analyses. "Father is the other of son, and son the other of father, and each only *is* as this other of the other; and at the same time, the one determination only is, in relation to the other; their being is a single subsistence" (1969:441).

The structure of double negativity, which sustains identity-in-difference by simultaneously distinguishing and reconciling opposites, is, in the final analysis, both infinite and absolute. Through double negation or self-referential negativity, opposites relate *to themselves* in otherness. Viewed speculatively, absolute negativity is not only the ground of difference but also establishes infinite unity. The reason Hegel describes this unity of opposites as infinite is that neither member of the relationship is burdened by unreconciled otherness. When negativity is adequately grasped in its infinity and absoluteness, it reveals itself to be the essence, the *Wesen* or *Inbegriff* of everything. Essence is pure negative activity that relates itself to itself in otherness. "The reflection-into-self," therefore, "is equally reflection-into-another, and vice versa" (1968b:par. 121). The other through which essence realizes itself is appearance. Hegel contends that "essence is not *behind* or *beyond* appearance" (1968b:par. 131). Rather, appearance is the manifestation or revelation of essence; it is essence in its existence. Essence realizes itself through active self-negation in which it posits itself as other, that is as determinate being, and returns to itself from this otherness by negating its own negation. Concrete particularity is the *Par-ousia*, the appearance of essence, the embodiment or *incarnation* of essentiality. When determinate being is comprehended as the self-determination of essential negativity, it is re-collected or resurrected in the eternity of substantial becoming. Through this process, essence becomes actual and actuality becomes essential. In theological language, God reveals himself through the incarnate Word. In the eternal life-process of spirit, Father becomes incarnate in Son, and Son is resurrected in Father. This Son, of course, is not merely a particular historical figure, but is universal human selfhood. Spirit inspires spirit, and spirit enlivens Spirit. From this perspective, God is no longer "afar off," the self no longer lost in "slumberous" solitude. The divine is reborn in self, even as self is reborn in the divine. But such redemption can be found only in time and history and is open to no one (not even God) who does not pass through "Death's door" and "lay down in the grave."/9/

It seems to me to be undeniable that the specter of nihilism haunts much twentieth-century experience and reflection. Historical events that extend from the ovens of Europe to the baked deserts of today's Africa have conspired to call into question the patterns and norms by which many generations have interpreted their world and lived their lives. Though many of our greatest artists and philosophers have been preoccupied with spiritual dissolution, theologians too often have been unwilling to confront this matter directly. We have seen that the response to the loss of center ranges from anxiety and dismay to joy and affirmation. Deconstruction, that movement of thought which today is commanding so much attention, might best be understood as post-modernism raised to method. By developing insights of Nietzsche, this movement apparently provides a way out of our impasse by offering a respectable, indeed a pleasurable transformation of necessity into virtue. To dialectical vision, however, this "gay wisdom" appears to be a variation of the unhappy consciousness that seems to be the fate of post-modern man. One can agree with Derrida's criticism of a metaphysics which venerates atemporal being or presence at the expense of temporal becoming without accepting his virtual absolutizing of absence. The metaphysics of presence and the metaphysics of absence *both* end in nihilism: the former resolves time in eternity, the latter dissolves eternity in time. Neither point of view, therefore, is sufficiently dialectical to capture the ambiguous interplay of continuity and discontinuity in human experience. Hegel's analysis of negativity establishes the internal relation of identity and difference in a way that discloses the absence in presence without losing presence in absence. From this point of view, we can begin to imagine how a new understanding of selfhood might incorporate a new understanding of God. The death of the transcendent Father need not be the complete disappearance of God, but can be seen as the birth of the divine, which now is grasped as an immanent and eternal process of dialectical development. The death of solitary selfhood need not be the total disappearance of self, but it can be seen as the birth of universal selfhood in which each becomes itself by relation to all. Moreover theology and anthropology no longer can be held apart, for we now recognize that these are but two aspects of a single problem. To work out the implications of the position I am suggesting will require a reexamination of some of our most basic philosophical and theological presuppositions. The journey along this way will be a difficult one. As Hegel points out, spirit, be it human or divine, "is not the life that shrinks from death and keeps itself untouched by devastation, but rather [is] the life that endures [death] and maintains itself in it. It wins its truth only when, in utter dismemberment, it finds itself" (1977:19). At present no other way seems open, for one who has gazed into the empty mirror can never regard God or self as he did before.

Notes

/1/   It is also important to note that Wittgenstein's interpretation of language anticipates central features of this view of human linguisticality.

/2/   It is, of course, obvious that pattern and meaning can be regarded as inherent in and not imposed upon nature and history. While originally rooted in religious belief, modern science would be impossible apart from the assumption of intrinsic order. It is not possible in this context to follow the origin and dissolution of the scientific community's views of natural order. It must suffice to point to the extraordinary significance of developments such as Heisenberg's uncertainty principle, relativity theory, and sub-atomic physics. It should also be noted that the hermeneutical problems we are considering involve important implications for the epistemology of science that only recently have been recognized.

/3/   This is Roland Barthes's phrase.

/4/   The literary dimensions of these developments are explored in M. L. Abrams's study of Romantic literature, *Natural Supernaturalism: Tradition and Revolution in Romantic Literature* (New York: W. W. Norton and Co., 1971).

/5/   This is Wallace Stevens's term.

/6/   We will explore the hermeneutical implications of this insight in what follows.

/7/   Though Derrida does not refer to Hegel in this context, the position on this issue which is developed in *Speech and Phenomena* is anticipated by Hegel in his account of "sense certainty" in the *Phenomenology*.

/8/   Although based on very different premises, Derrida's conclusions bear marked similarity to Hume's interpretation of personal identity. See: *A Treatise on Human Nature* (London: John Noon, 1739), "Appendix."

/9/   Blake, *Milton*, 32:40.

Works Consulted

Altizer, Thomas
    1967   *The New Apocalypse: The Radical Christian Vision of William Blake*. East Lansing: Michigan State University Press.

1979   *The Descent Into Hell: A Study of Radical Reversal of the Christian Consciousness*. New York: Seabury.

Barthes, Roland
1979   "From Work to Text," *Textual Strategies: Perspectives in Post-Structuralist Criticism*. Ed. Josué V. Harari. Ithaca: Cornell University Press.

Crossan, John Dominic
1980   *Cliffs of Fall: Paradox and Polyvalence in the Parables of Jesus*. New York: Seabury.

Culler, Jonathan
1975   *Structuralist Poetics: Structuralism, Linguistics, and the Study of Literature*. Ithaca: Cornell University Press.

De Man, Paul
1974   "Nietzsche's Theory of Rhetoric," *Symposium*. Vol. XXVIII, no. 1.

Derrida, Jacques
1973   *Speech and Phenomena and Other Essays on Husserl's Theory of Signs*. Trans. D. B. Allison. Evanston: Northwestern University Press.
1978   *Writing and Difference*. Trans. A. Bass. Chicago: University of Chicago Press.

Foucault, Michel
1969   *L'Archeologie du savoir*. Paris.
1970   *The Order of Things: An Archaeology of the Human Sciences*. New York: Random House.
1979   "What is an Author?" *Textual Strategies: Perspectives in Post-Structuralist Criticism*. Ed. Jousé V. Harari. Ithaca: Cornell University Press.

Hegel, G. W. F.
1968a   *Lectures on the History of Philosophy*. Trans. E. S. Haldane. Volume I. New York: Humanities Press.
1968b   *The Logic of Hegel*. Trans. W. Wallace. New York: Oxford University Press.
1969   *Science of Logic*. Trans. A. V. Miller. New York: Humanities Press.
1977   *Phenomenology of Spirit*. Trans. A. V. Miller. New York: Oxford University Press.

Heidegger, Martin
1957   *Der Satz vom Grund*. Pfullingen.

Kant, I.
1963   "What is Enlightenment?" *On History*. Trans. L. W. Beck. New York: Bobbs-Merrill.

Lévi-Strauss, Claude
1962   *La Pensée sauvage*. Paris.

Malraux, André
1960   *The Metamorphosis of the Gods*. Trans. S. Gilbert. New York: Doubleday.

Miller, J. Hillis
1963   *The Disappearance of God: Five Nineteenth Century Writers*. Cambridge: Harvard University Press.

Nietzsche, F.
1957   *Thus Spoke Zarathustra*. Trans. M. Cowan. Chicago: Henry Regnery.
1966   *Beyond Good and Evil*. Trans. W. Kaufmann. New York: Vintage Books.

Said, Edward
1975   *Beginnings: Intention and Method*. New Basic Books.

Sartre, Jean-Paul
1955   *No-Exit*. Trans. L. Abel. New York: Vintage Books.
1964   *Nausea*. Trans. L. Alexander. New York: New Directions.

Saussure, F.
1959   *Course in General Linguistics*. Trans. W. Baskin. New York: Philosophical Library.

G N I C A R T
T R A C I N G
Inter Alios
Mark C. Taylor

1.

Trace: A visible mark or sign of the former presence or passage of some person, thing, or event; vestige, track, trail. To follow the footprints of. To copy by following the lines of the original drawing on a transparent sheet placed upon it. To plait, twine, interweave.

Tracing: Drawing. Dancing. Following, *Imitatio*. Interweaving: one becoming two, or three, or . . . , while remaining one. An identity-in-difference and a difference-in-identity.

2.

To trace is to follow, copy, imitate, represent. Tracing represents by forming an image, an *imago* which is both identical with and different from the traced. Representation presents by absenting and absents by presenting. Tracing, therefore, simultaneously reveals and conceals the origin-al.

3.

If trace is vicar, then representation is vicarious satisfaction—sublation is sublimation.

4.

"The presence-absence of the trace . . . carries in itself the problems of the letter and the spirit, of body and soul. . . . All dualisms, all theories of the immortality of the soul or of the spirit, as well as all monisms, spiritualist or materialist . . . are the unique theme of a metaphysics whose entire history was compelled to strive toward the reduction of the trace."

o o o o o

5.

Our task is to undo the theology of presence and the philosophy of absence with a hermeneutics of word. The theology of identity and the philosophy of difference join in a philosophical theology and theological philosophy of identity-in-difference and difference-in-identity.

6.

"Dialectics is apocalypse; reversal; wakening from the dead."
.Noisrevnoc si hcihw noisrevni eht si noisiv citpylacopa

7.

The principle of noncontradiction is the cross upon which Albion hangs. "The Pentecostal darkness: the sun shall be turned to darkness. To overcome the opposition of darkness and light, cleanliness and dirt, order and chaos; the marriage of heaven and hell. To seduce the world to madness. Christ is within the wall of paradise, which is the wall of the law of contradiction; and the destruction of the law of contradiction is the supreme task of higher logic."

8.

Identity *is* difference and difference *is* identity. "In other words, identity is the reflection-into-self that is identity only as internal repulsion, and is this repulsion as reflection-into-self, repulsion which immediately takes itself back into itself. Thus it is identity as difference that is identical with itself. But difference is only identical with itself in so far as it is not identity but absolute non-identity. But non-identity is absolute in so far as it contains nothing of its other but only itself, that is, in so far as it is absolute identity with itself. Identity, therefore, is *in its own self* absolute non-identity. But it is also the *determination* of identity as against non-identity. . . . Difference in itself is self-related difference; as such it is the negativity of itself, the difference not of an other, but *of itself from itself*; it is not itself but its other. But that which is different from difference is identity. Difference is therefore itself and identity. Both together constitute difference; it is the whole, and its moment."

9.

Otherness is not merely other, difference is not indifferent. "Apart from the self-embodiment of otherness, identity could not stand out from itself, hence self-identity would be neither manifest nor actual. Nor can self-identity appear and be real apart from identity's own embodiment in otherness."

10.

Seeing the yes in the no and the no in the yes is the discovery that affirmation is negation and negation is affirmation. "The determinations which constitute the positive and negative consist . . . in the fact that the positive and negative are . . . absolute *moments* of the opposition; their subsistence is inseparably *one* reflection; it is a single mediation in which each *is* through the non-being of its other, and so *is* through its other or its own non-being. . . . In the first place, then, each *is, only in so far as the other is*; it is what it is, through the other, through its own non-being; it is only a *positedness*; secondly, it is, *in so far as the other is not*; it is what it is, through the non-being of the other; it is *reflection-into-self*. But these two are the *one* mediation of the opposition as such, in which they are simply only *posited moments*."

11.

Nihilism is the inability to see positivity in negativity, presence in absence. Dogmatism is the inability to see negativity in positivity, absence in presence. Vision is the ability to see positivity in negativity and negativity in positivity, presence in absence and absence in presence.

12.

You cannot name God without naming Satan. Satan is called Opacity; God, Transparency.

13.

To see is to see into; genuine sight is always in-sight. To see into is to see through, through to the indwelling other. "Here, every given identity must pass into its own intrinsic opposite, must become its own inherent other, if apocalyptic reversal is to occur. Such a reversal is not a literal negation of the reality which it affects, it is rather a total transformation of the meaning and actuality of that reality, thereby allowing it to evolve into a wholly new form and identity."

14.
A(R)MO(U)R

The agony of identity and difference is host-ility. "Our enemy our host who feeds us." *Corpus Mysticum: Parasitos* and *Hostia* joined in Holy Communion. *Hoc est corpus meum*. Hocus-pocus: hostility becomes love. "Eucharist is the marriage feast; the union of the bridegroom and the bride." The wedding of identity and difference is the hierogamy which is hierophantic.

o o o o o

15.

A trace is a mark; Mark, a trace. Tracing is marking; Marking, tracing.
". . . the self of the living present is primordially a trace."

16.

"Beneath the bottoms of the Graves, which is Earth's
        central joint,
There is a place where Contrarieties are equally true. . . ."

17.

"Selving"

"I am the strife
    For the strife is just this conflict,
        Which is not any indifference of the two as diverse,
    But is their being bound together.
I am not the one of these two
    Taking part in the strife,
        But am both the combatants
    And the strife itself.
I am the fire and the water
    Which touch one another . . .
        The collision and the unity of what flies apart . . .
    Of what is now separated,
                        Fragmented,
And now is reconciled in unity with itself."

18.

Selfhood is *agon*, selving agony. Selves struggle to join the opposites
they are. The more vital the self, the deeper the opposites. Contradiction is
the universal life-pulse.

19.

The self is "a relation which relates itself to its own self, and in relating
itself to its own self, relates itself to another"—an other within and an other
without. Relation to the other within turns everything upside down, and the

relation to the other without turns everything inside out. Upside down and inside out: madness—or salvation.

20.

Instead of "to be *or* not to be," the sum of the matter is to be *and* not to be, for to be is not to be, and not to be is to be. "Let those who insist that being and nothing are different tackle the problem of stating in what the difference consists." My identity *is* my difference, and my difference *is* my identity.

21.

"Now presence becomes absence, and becomes actual as absence, and that absence is the self-enactment of presence. Therefore presence can now be actual only in its absence, in its absence from itself, from its own self-identity." My presence *is* an absence, and my absence *is* a presence.

22.

Question: "Have you noticed that only in time of illness or disaster or death are people real?"

Answer: Death is the absence in the presence of which the self becomes itself.

23.

A fundamental theological puzzle for our time:

Is **O** empty or full?

Bindu: zero *or* semen; zero *and* semen.

Nada and *Niente* derive from *Nasci*.

° ° ° ° °

24.

The question is no longer how the Word redeems, but how to redeem the Word.

25.

Optical Allusions: Hieroglyphics as Hierophany.

Ground grounds figure—figure turns from and returns to ground. Only so is figure ground-ed. Yet a figureless ground is groundless. Ground, therefore, is figural. Figure grounds ground. Figure(s) ground(s) figure(s) ground(s) figure(s) ground(s) . . .

26.

"The relation of ground and grounded becomes an external form imposed on the content which is indifferent to these determinations. But in point of fact the two are not external to one another; for the content is this, to be the *identity* of the *ground* with itself in the *grounded*, and of the *grounded* in the *ground*. The side of the ground has shown that it is itself a posited, and the side of the grounded that it is itself ground; each is in itself this identity of the whole."

27.

White space is the emptiness which surrounds and invades the word. Without white
space, there is only darkness, invisibility.
Black space is the fullness which surrounds

and invades the wordless. Without dark
space, there is only light, invisibility.
Word reveals the fullness of emptiness and
the   emptiness   of   fullness.   Writing   is
scripture, the play, or the interplay of
white   space   and   black   space   which
enlightens by bringing darkness to light
and light to darkness. Words or Golgotha.

28.

The negative is positive and the positive is negative.

29.

"To say that madness is dazzlement is to say that the madman sees the daylight, the same daylight as the man of reason (both live in the same brightness); but seeing this same daylight, and nothing but this daylight and nothing in it, he sees it as void, as night, as nothing; for him the shadows are the way to perceive daylight. Which means that, seeing the night and the nothingness of the night, he does not see at all. And believing he sees, he admits as realities the hallucinations of his imagination and all the multitudinous population of the night. That is why delirium and dazzlement are in a relation which constitutes the essence of madness, exactly as truth and light, in their fundamental relation, constitute classical reason."

30.

"Is not the body's erotic zone where the garment leaves gaps?" The textuality of sexuality.

31.

"Dreams attest that we constantly mean something other than what we say; in dreams the manifest meaning endlessly refers to hidden meaning; that is what makes every dreamer a poet. From this point of view, dreams express the private archeology of the dreamer, which at times coincides with that of entire peoples. . . . The analyst interprets this account, substituting for it another text which is, in his eyes, the thought-content of desire, i.e., what desire would say could it speak without restraint." The sexuality of textuality.

32.

Language games: Language is a game—we the players. We play the game and the game plays us. But what kind of a game is this? It is a game of hide-and-seek. Who, then, is it? Rather what is it, es, id?

33.

Homo linguisticus: We make the game and the game makes us. Making it and being made. Playing the game, we play with ourselves. Language is autoerotic—masturbation. *Homo linguisticus* is *Homo* homo. Be careful not to get caught when you are playing hide-and-seek. Daddy will cut id off, or tell you to be silent. Wait until Abba is gone to play. Speech comes when "Nobodaddy" is gone—He is dead when word(s) come.

34.

Logos Spermatikos: Semen-ial, seminary words to be dis-seminated. The flow of creative juices. "The word *cerebral* is from the same root as Ceres, goddess of cereals, of growth and fertility; the same root as *cresco*, to grow, and *creo*, to create. Onians, archaeologist of language, who uncovers lost worlds of meaning, buried meanings, has dug up a prehistoric image of the body, according to which head and genital intercommunicate via the spinal column: the gray matter of the brain, the spinal marrow, and the seminal fluid are all one identical substance, on tap in the genital and stored in the head." White be-coming gray be-coming black. Penis as pen and pen as pen-is.

35.

[W]rite: The *archē* of forgetting is fore-getting. The *telos* of remembering is re-membering. Ritual enacts a play of forgetting and remembering. On the one hand, rituals are necessary because we forget, possible because we remember. On the other hand, rituals are necessary because we remember, possible because we forget. Writual is the dramatic struggle to present the absent and to absent the present.

36.

"To make in ourselves a new consciousness, an erotic sense of reality, is to become conscious of symbolism. Symbolism is mind making connections (correspondences) rather than distinctions (separations). Symbolism makes conscious interconnections and unions that were unconscious and repressed. Freud says, symbolism is on the track [is a trace] of a former identity, a lost unity: the lost continent, Atlantis, underneath the sea of life in which we live enisled; or perhaps even our union with the sea (Thalassa); oceanic consciousness; the unity of the whole cosmos as one living creature, as Plato said in the *Timaeus*."

37.

Spacing is a caesurean birth. "Trace is the opening of the first exteriority in general, the enigmatic relationship of the living to its other and of an inside to an outside: spacing."

38.

Blanks, gaps, holes are not empty, but are full, whole, holey. "Between the letters and the lines, and all around the blank margins, the spirit circulates freely. . . ."

39.

Satan is called Opacity, God is named Transparency. "Transparency. To let the light not on but in or through. To look not at the thing but through it; to see between the lines; to see language as lace, black on white; or white on black as in the sky at night, or in the space on which dreams are traced."

o   o   o   o   o

40.

Silence is the white space, voice the black space of speech. "In a dialectical view: silence and speech, these two, are one."

41.

"The silence of silence comes to an end in the presence of speech, as the actuality of speech shatters silence, embodying in its pure otherness a silence which is the other of itself. Silence cannot simply be silent in the presence of speech, for silence speaks in the voice of speech, and speaks in that self-negating otherness which embodies itself in its own otherness. Silence as silence is absent in speech, but silence is present as the 'other' of speech, and in that presence it embodies a new identity of itself."

42.

If *nothing* can be said, then how can we hear the unsaid? "A raid on the inarticulate" can be mounted only if nothing *can* be said.

43.

Silenus, leader of the satyrs, is the foster-father of Bacchus. Silence is the Bacchanalian revel which awakens the dreamer from "Newton's sleep" to twofold, threefold, fourfold vision.

44.

To hear silence is to see gaps. The prophet and the analyst know that for those who have ears to hear and eyes to see, there is no literal truth. "To let the silence in is symbolism."

o o o o o

45.

"The meaning is not in the words but between the words, in the silence; forever beyond the reach, the rape, of literal-minded explication; forever inviolate, forever new; the still unravished bride of quietness. The virgin womb of the imagination in which the word becomes flesh is silence; and she remains a virgin."

46.

Meaning is relative or relational. It arises from the play, the interplay of identity and difference, presence and absence, light and darkness, voice and silence.

47.

If, as the poet claims, "things are because of interrelations, interactions," then "meaning is not in things but in between; in the iridescence, the interplay; in the interconnections; at the intersections, at the crossroads. Meaning is transitional as it is transitory; in the puns or bridges, the correspondence."

48.

"Dans la langue il n'y a que des differences sans termes positifs." In other words, "As far as a language is concerned, it is the lateral relation of one sign to another which makes each of them significant, so that meaning appears only at the intersection of and as it were in the interval between words." Meaningful intercourse.

49.

The contextuality of meaning and the meaningfulness of context disclose the texture of texts. Texts are fabric-actions woven from texts. The warp and woof of textual interweaving is tracing.

o o o o o

50.

A design: To de-sign

"To design is to cut a trace. Most of us know the word 'sign' only in its debased meaning—lines on a surface. But we can make a design also when we cut a furrow into the soil to open it to seed and growth. The design is the whole of the traits of that drawing which structures and prevails throughout the open, unlocked freedom of language. The design is the drawing of the being of language, the structure of a show in which are joined the speakers and their speaking: what is spoken and what of it is unspoken in all that is given in the speaking."

51.

Dialectical reversal turns inside out and outside in. Subject and object are inseparably bound in a relation of coimplication in which each becomes itself through the other. To know, therefore, is "to have the outside inside and to be inside the outside."

52.

In poetic language, the universe of discourse *becomes* the discourse of the universe. According to Malraux, Renoir's "vision was less a way of looking at the sea than the secret elaboration of a world to which that depth of blue whose immensity he was recapturing pertained."

53.

Vision is synesthetic: a seeing which is a saying and a saying which is a seeing.

54.

To hear the Word is to see. "The parables of Jesus are circumspections of the horizon or horizons of things. This is the reason the details of the narrative picture, though set out with intense realism, cannot be pressed: they invite attention, not to themselves, but to the horizon, just as the painting leads our eye unfalteringly to the vanishing point [i.e., the *bindu*]. Of the painting, for instance, of the animals painted on the walls of Lascaux, Merleau-Ponty writes: 'It is more accurate to say that I see according to it, or with it, than that I *see it.*' The parable and the painting draw the eye, by means of a skillfully arranged soft focus on objects in the foreground, to the horizon by virtue of which those objects gain their places and faces. Thus, the objects in the foreground previously released again become the object of attention, but within a new horizon and undergirded and protected by fresh integrity."

° ° ° ° °

55.

Metaphor is a cross—of identity and difference, presence and absence, voice and silence. Metaphorical vision is *stereopsis*: seeing identity-in-difference and difference-in-identity, pluralized unity and unified plurality. To see metaphorically is to become cross-eyed.

56.

"In order that a metaphor obtains, one must continue to identify the previous incompatibility *through* the new compatibility [Transparency]. 'Remoteness' is preserved within 'proximity.' To see *the like* is to see the same in spite of, and through, the different. This tension between sameness and difference characterizes the logical structure of likeness."

57.

The category of "metaphor" is neither noetic nor ontological, but is onto-noetic. "Metaphor and symbol serve to carry over into consciousness the carrying over between things, and between things and the self, in their very being."

58.

A metaphysics of metaphor is a metaphysics of "final participation" whose object is to object to the object, without being subject to the subject.

59.

Metaphor is born of that higher logic which shatters the law of noncontradiction. "Logic is only slavery within the bounds of language. Language has within it, however, an illogical element, the metaphor. Its principal force brings about an identification of the nonidentical; it is thus an operation of the imagination."

60.

As transitional language μεταφωρά carries the old over to the new, and speaks the new through the old. Thus the metaphor conceals even while revealing, and reveals even while concealing. Metaphorical language is always *"sous rature."*

61.

Jesus   ⨯   God.

62.

Metaphor is the language of the frontiersman, the path-finder who seeks the trail, searches the traces which lead from this world to the next. "One should meditate upon all of the following together: writing as the possibility of the road and of difference, the history of writing and the history of the road, of the rupture, of the *via rupta*, of the path that is broken, beaten, *fracta*, of the space of reversibility and of repetition traced by the opening, the divergence from, and the violent spacing of nature, of the natural, savage, salvage, forest. The *silva* is savage, the *via rupta* is written, discerned, and inscribed violently as the difference, as form imposed on the *hyle*, in the forest, in wood as matter. . . ."

63.

"In an *Ndembu* ritual context, almost every article used, every gesture employed, every song or prayer, every unit of space and time, by convention stands for something other than itself. It is more than it seems, and often a good deal more. The Ndembu are aware of the expressive or symbolic function of ritual elements. A ritual element or unit is called *chijikijilu*. Literally, this word signifies a 'landmark' or 'blaze.' Its etymon is *ku-jikijila*, 'to blaze a trail'—by slashing a mark on a tree with an ax or breaking one of its branches. This term is drawn originally from the technical vocabulary of hunting, a vocabulary heavily invested with ritual beliefs and practices. *Chijikijilu* also means a 'beacon,' a conspicuous feature of the landscape, such as an ant hill, which distinguishes one man's gardens or one chief's realm from another's. Thus, it has two main significations: (1) as a *hunter's blaze* it represents an element of connection between known and unknown territory, for it is by a chain of such elements that a hunter finds his way back from the unfamiliar bush to the familiar village; (2) as both *blaze* and *beacon* it conveys the notion of the structured and ordered as against the unstructured and chaotic. Its ritual use is already metaphorical: it connects the known world of sensorily perceptible phenomena with the unknown and invisible realm of the shades. It makes intelligible what is mysterious, and also dangerous."

64.

Metaphor is blaze, fire—"Apocalypse Now"—realized eschatology. The apocalyptic world is the world of "total metaphor." For the seer, "The whole creation will be consumed and appear infinite and holy, whereas it now appears finite and corrupt."

65.

Parable is "expanded metaphor," "the linguistic incarnation." Παρα βολή: "'Para' is a double antithetical prefix signifying at once proximity and distance, similarity and difference, interiority and exteriority, something inside a domestic economy and at the same time outside it, something simultaneously this side of a boundary line, threshold, or margin, and also beyond it, equivalent in status and also secondary or subsidiary, submissive, as of guest to host, slave to master. A thing in 'para', moreover, is not only simultaneously on both sides of the boundary line between inside and out. It is also the boundary itself, the screen which is a permeable membrane connecting inside and outside. It confuses them with one another, allowing the outside in, making the inside out, dividing them and joining them. It also forms an ambiguous transition between one and the other."

66.

Parable: "an ambiguous transition between one and another." The parable projects a world into which it attempts to translate the hearer. "Since the world it describes deforms the 'received' world, it constitutes nothing less than an invitation to live in that world, to see the world in that way, to take up one's abode within a totality of significations that is different from the everyday world."

67.

Reading a parable, therefore, is a *meta phora*, a passage, a journey a pilgrimage. *Imitatio*: to follow the footprints of.

68.

"One is inside
then outside what one has been inside,
One feels empty
because there is nothing inside oneself
One tries to get inside oneself
       that inside of the outside
       that one was once inside
       once one tries to get oneself inside what
       one is outside:
       to eat and to be eaten
to have the outside inside and to be
       inside the outside."

69.

As "visible inclusions of the alien in the sight of the familiar," metaphors and parables are imaginative without being imaginary. "Resemblance in metaphor is an activity of the imagination; and in metaphor the imagination is life."

70.

Imagination is the power of life and death—the means by which the absent becomes present and the present becomes absent.

71.

"Then Jesus appeared standing by Albion as the Good Shepherd
By the lost Sheep that he had found, & Albion knew that it
Was the Lord, the Universal Humanity; & Albion saw this Form
A Man, & they conversed as Man with Man in Ages of Eternity.
And the Divine Appearance was the likeness & similitude of Los."

72.

"God and the imagination are one."

73.

Metaphors and parables are stumbling-blocks to Jews and folly to Greeks. Only Frontiersmen, limen, magicians, passengers, and madmen speak in metaphors and parables. "It is for the other world that the madman sets sail in his fools' boat; it is from the other world that he comes when he disembarks. The madman's voyage is at once a rigorous diversion and an absolute Passage. In one sense, it simply develops across a half-real, half-imaginary geography, the madman's liminal position on the horizon of medieval concern—a position symbolized and made real at the same time by the madman's privilege of being *confined* within the city *gates*; his exclusion must enclose him; if he cannot and must not have another *prison* than the *threshold* itself, he is kept at the point of passage. He is put in the interior of the exterior, and inversely. A highly symbolic position, which will doubtless remain his until our own day, if we are willing to admit that what was formerly a visible fortress of order has now become the castle of our conscience."

74.

Madness. And yet, "there is no nonmetaphoric language to oppose to metaphors."

75.

"The antinomy between mind and body, word and deed, speech and silence, overcome. Everything is only a metaphor; there is only poetry."

o o o o o

76.

Poetry puts magic back into words. "Poetry is the establishment of Being by means of the word."

77.

POIESIS

"By the word of the Lord the heavens were made,
    and all their host by the breath of his mouth.

For he spoke, and it came to be;
  he commanded, and it stood forth."

78.

```
ABRACADABRA
 ABRACADABR
  ABRACADAB
   ABRACADA
    ABRACAD
     ABRACA
      ABRAC
       ABRA
        ABR
         AB
          A
```

Abracadabra, the magic word which discloses the magic of words, probably derives from Abraxas. $\alpha+\beta+\rho+\alpha+\xi+\alpha+s = 365$.

79.

Abraxas: *Ab ben rouach hakados; soteria apo xylou* (Father, Son, Spirit, Holy; Salvation from the cross); or *Anthropous ozon hagioi xyloi* (Saving mankind by the holy cross).

80.

The "Good Shepherd" who is the "shepherd of Being" is a "word magician." "The clearest evidence of Jesus' knowledge and use of magic is the eucharist, a magical rite of a familiar sort."

81.

The true magician crosses homeopathic and contagious magic, the metaphoric and the metonymic, the paradigmatic and the syntagmatic.

```
         S
         Y
         N
         C
  DIACHRONIC
         R
         O
         N
         I
         C
```

Magic is the union of time and eternity, "the marriage of heaven and hell." "The bird fights its way out of the egg. The egg is the world. Who would be born must first destroy a world. The bird flies to God. That God's name is

Abraxas. . . . Abraxas was the god who was both god and devil." "Fearful symmetry."

o o o o o

82.

A metaphor for metaphor: *Word.*

83.

We must begin with absence, with silence, with the confession of the absence of word(s). And we must dwell with this silence until we can hear, hear how absence presents. Then we shall see, see that the word is absent when present, and present when absent.

84.

The Road to Emmaus

When Jesus was present, he was absent, when absent, present. Why? Because he is Word.

On the road to Emmaus, Jesus' presence is absence, and his absence is presence. They see, but do not see; they hear only the silence of an empty tomb. "And when he had sat down with them at the table, he took bread and said the blessing; he broke the bread, and offered it to them. Then their eyes were opened, and they recognized him; and he vanished from their sight." *Hoc est corpus meum.* Hocus-pocus: a vanishing act that really opened their eyes! And what do they see? They see his presence in absence. But to do so, they must likewise see absence in their presence. To hear the Word is to see, to see the presence in absence which answers our absence in presence.

85.

"Dialectics is apocalypse, reversal; wakening from the dead." Begending: Genesis *is* Apocalypse *is* Genesis.

86.

"From the perspective of our own time, the eschatological call of Jesus initially appears as a nihilistic call to madness or to death." "Joining vision and blindness, image and judgment, hallucination and language, sleep and

waking, day and night, madness is ultimately nothing, for it unites in them
all that is negative. But the paradox of this *nothing* is to *manifest* itself, to
explode in signs, in words, in gestures. Inextricable unity of order and
disorder, of the reasonable being of things and this nothingness of madness!"

87.

"The goal cannot be the elimination of magical thinking, or madness;
the goal can only be conscious magic, or conscious madness; conscious
mastery of these fires. And dreaming while awake."

o o o o o

88.

Experimentum Crucis

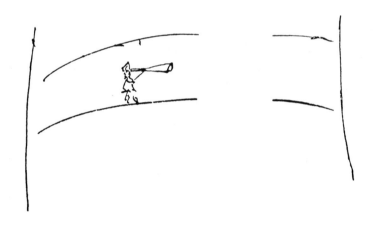

89.

Aphoristic language is gappy—full of holes. *L'espace blanc*. Silence and
speech "acting together." Form *is* content.

90.

"We shall now have a closer look at the basic function of the blank as
regards the guidance it exercises in the process of communication. As blanks
mark the suspension of connectability between textual segments, they simultaneously form a condition for the connection to be established. By definition,
however, they can clearly have no determinate content of their own. How,

then, is one to describe them? As an empty space they are nothing in themselves, and yet as a 'nothing' they are a vital propellant for initiating communication." "Whenever the reader bridges the gaps, communication begins."

91.

Aphorisms form a workbook that is a workspace in which all authorship is joint authorship. "Every text, being itself the intertext of another text, belongs to the intertextual, which must not be confused with the text's origins: to search for the 'sources of' and 'influence upon' a work is to satisfy the myth of filiation. The quotations from which a text is constructed are anonymous, irrecoverable, and yet *already read*: they are quotations without quotation marks. . . . Thus . . . the text might well take as its motto the words of the man possessed by devils: 'My name is legion, for we are many.'"

92.

"The Text is plural. This does not mean just that it has several meanings, but rather that it achieves plurality of meaning, an *irreducible* plurality. The Text is not the coexistence of meanings but passage, traversal [*Metaphora*]; thus it answers not to an interpretation, liberal though it may be, but to an explosion, a dissemination. The Text's plurality does not depend on the ambiguity of its contents, but rather on what could be called the *stereographic plurality* of the signifiers that weave it. . . ."

93.

Writing is tracing, interweaving which is fabrication. The fabric of the text, however, always has loose ends. Ever unfinished, the text is a "permanent metamorphosis" which transforms reader into author and author into reader.

94.

Aphoristic writing clears a space for Alios to Inter.

o o o o o

95.

"Few are experienced enough in the
difference between an object of
scholarship and a matter of thought."

o o o o o

Works Consulted

Altizer, Thomas J. J.
1967 *The New Apocalypse: The Radical Christian Vision of William Blake.* Michigan State University Press.
1977 *The Self-Embodiment of God.* New York: Harper & Row.
1979 *The Descent Into Hell: A Study of the Radical Reversal of the Christian Consciousness.* New York: Seabury Press.

Barb, A. A.
1957 "Abraxas-studien." *Hommages à Waldemar Deonna.* Bruxelles.

Barfield, Owen
1957 *Saving the Appearances: A Study in Idolatry.* London: Faber and Faber.

Barthes, Roland
1979 "From Work to Text." *Textual Strategies: Perspectives in Post-Structuralist Criticism.* Ed. J. V. Harari. Ithaca: Cornell University Press.

Blake, William
1974 *The Illuminated Blake.* Ed. D. V. Erdman. New York: Doubleday.

Brown, Norman O.
1968 *Love's Body.* New York: Random House.

Culler, Jonathan
1975 *Structuralist Poetics: Structuralism, Linguistics and the Study of Literature.* Ithaca: Cornell University Press.
1976 *Ferdinand de Saussure.* New York: Penguin.

Derrida, Jacques
1973 *Speech and Phenomena and Other Essays on Husserl's Theory of Signs.* Trans. D. B. Allison. Evanston: Northwestern University Press.
1976 *Of Grammatology.* Trans. G. C. Spivak. Baltimore: Johns Hopkins University Press.
1978 *Writing and Difference.* Trans. A. Bass. Chicago: University of Chicago Press.
1979 "The Supplement of Copula: Philosophy *before* Linguistics." *Textual Strategies: Perspectives in Post-Structuralist Criticism.* Ed. J. V. Harari. Ithaca: Cornell University Press.

Foucault, Michel
1975 *Madness and Civilization: A History of Insanity in the Age of Reason.* Trans. R. Howard. New York: Random House.

Funk, Robert W.
1966 *Language, Hermeneutic, and Word of God.* New York: Harper & Row.
1975 *Jesus as Precursor.* Missoula: Scholars Press.

Hegel, G. W. F.
   1968   *Lectures on the Philosophy of Religion*. Trans. E. B. Speirs
                     and J. B. Sanderson. New York: Humanities Press.
   1968   *Hegel's Science of Logic*. Trans. A. V. Miller. New York:
                     Humanities Press.
   1977   *Phenomenology of Spirit*. Trans. A. V. Miller. New York:
                     Oxford University Press.

Hart, Ray L.
   1968   *Unfinished Man and the Imagination: Toward an Ontology
                     and a Rhetoric of Revelation*. New York: Herder and Herder.

Heidegger, Martin
   1966   *Discourse on Thinking*. Trans. J. M. Anderson and E. H.
                     Freund. New York: Harper & Row.
   1971   *On the Way to Language*. Trans. P. Hertz. New York: Harper
                     & Row.
   1971   *Poetry, Language, Thought*. Trans. A. Hofstader. New York:
                     Harper & Row.
   1973   *The End of Philosophy*. Trans. J. Stambaugh. New York:
                     Harper & Row.

Hesse, Hermann
   1970   *Demian: The Story of Emil Sinclair's Youth*. Trans. M. Roloff
                     and M. Lebeck. New York: Bantam Books.

Iser, Wolfgang
   1978   *The Act of Reading: A Theory of Aesthetic Response*.
                     Baltimore: Johns Hopkins University Press.

Kazantzakis, Nikos
   1965   *The Last Temptation of Christ*. Trans. P. A. Bien. New York:
                     Bantam Books.

Kierkegaard, Søren
   1970   *The Sickness Unto Death*. Trans. W. Lowrie. Princeton:
                     Princeton University Press.

Laing, R. D.
   1970   *Knots*. New York: Random House.

Merleau-Ponty, Maurice
   1964   *Sense and Non-Sense*. Trans. H. L. Dreyfus and P. A.
                     Dreyfus. Evanston: Northwestern University Press.
   1964   *Signs*. Trans. R. C. McCleary. Evanston: Northwestern
                     University Press.
   1968   *The Visible and the Invisible*. Trans. A. Lingis. Evanston:
                     Northwestern University Press.

Miller, J. Hillis
   1979   "The Critic as Host." *Deconstruction and Criticism*. New
                     York: Seabury.

Nietzsche, Friedrich
   1910 ff.   *Complete Works*. Ed. O. Levy. London: Allen and Unwin.

Percy, Walker
    1961   *The Moviegoer*. New York: Knopf.
Raschke, Carl A.
    1979   *The Alchemy of the Word: Language and the End of Theology*. Missoula: Scholars Press.
Ricoeur, Paul
    1970   *Freud and Philosophy: An Essay on Interpretation*. Trans. D. Savage. New Haven: Yale University Press.
    1976   *Interpretation Theory: Discourse and the Surplus of Meaning*. Fort Worth: Texas Christian University Press.
    1978   "The Metaphorical Process as Cognition, Imagination, and Feeling." *Critical Inquiry* 5/1:143–59.
Rosen, Stanley
    1969   *Nihilism: A Philosophical Essay*. New Haven: Yale University Press.
Stevens, Wallace
    1951   *The Necessary Angel: Essays on Reality and the Imagination*. New York: Knopf.
    1957   *Opus Posthumous*. Ed. S. F. Morse. New York: Knopf.
    1972   *The Collected Poems of Wallace Stevens*. New York: Knopf.
Smith, Morton
    1978   *Jesus the Magician*. New York: Harper & Row.
Taylor, Mark C.
    1980   *Journeys to Selfhood: Hegel and Kierkegaard*. Berkeley: University of California Press.
Turbayne, Colin
    1970   *The Myth of Metaphor*. Columbia: University of South Carolina Press.
Turner, Victor
    1969   *The Ritual Process: Structure and Anti-Structure*. Chicago: Aldine Publishing Co.